Finding
Wales

In Memory of
Siân Busby
Tony Fielden
Alan Rees

Finding
Wales

Reflections of Returning Exiles

Peter Daniels

y Lolfa

Many thanks to the following for letting me tell their stories:

Alan Litherland, Enid Morris, Geoff Griffiths, Peter Lane, Llew Thomas, Gillian from Newport, Tony Jenkins, Roger Banner, Huw Jones, Richard Davies, Peter Williams, Cledwyn Davies, Rhian Jones, Iain Richards

And to editors Eifion Jenkins and Carolyn Hodges, for their support and advice.

First impression: 2017

Cover design: Y Lolfa

ISBN: 978 1 78461 445 4

Published and printed in Wales
on paper from well-maintained forests by
Y Lolfa Cyf., Talybont, Ceredigion SY24 5HE
website www.ylolfa.com
e-mail ylolfa@ylolfa.com
tel 01970 832 304
fax 832 782

Contents

Acknowledgements

I WOULD LIKE to thank the following authors and publishers for permission to incorporate lengthy quotations from their named works:

- J Geraint Jenkins, *Life and Traditions in Rural Wales* (World Conference on Records, 1980)
- Harold Carter, *Against the Odds* (Institute of Welsh Affairs, 2010)
- Jon Gower, *The Story of Wales* (BBC Books 2012); *Real Llanelli* (Seren, 2009)
- Siôn T Jobbins, *The Phenomenon of Welshness* (Carreg Gwalch, 2011); *The Phenomenon of Welshness II* (Carreg Gwalch, 2013)
- Byron Rogers, *Three Journeys* (Gomer, 2011)
- Imogen Rhia Herrad, *Beyond the Pampas, In Search of Patagonia* (Seren, 2012)
- Dan Boucher, *The Big Society in a Small Country* (Institute of Welsh Affairs, 2013)
- Selma Chalabi, *In Search of a 21st Century Welsh Identity, Eye on Wales* (BBC Radio Wales, July 2011)

I have also included short individual quotes or references from the following:

Alun Richards (*Carwyn*, Christopher Davies 2002), Ned Thomas (*The Welsh Extremist*, Y Lolfa 1973), Trevor Fishlock (*Wales and the Welsh*, Cassell 1972), David Williams (*A History of Modern Wales*, John Murray 1951), Martin Shipton (*Poor Man's Parliament*, Seren 2011), John Davies (*A History of Wales*, Penguin Books 2007), Noah Hawley (*The Good Father*, Hodder 2012), Ray Gravelle (*Grav*, Gomer 2009), Alun Gibbard (*Delme Thomas*, Y Lolfa 2014), WalesOnline (*Meet Brechfa*, 22 Jan 2013), Owen Sheers (*Calon*, Faber & Faber 2013), Jan Morris

(*Wales: Epic Views of a Small Country,* Oxford 1985), Pamela Petro (*Travels in an Old Tongue,* London 1997), Gareth Payne, Rebecca Payne, Daniel Farewell (*BMJ,* Dec 2008), Roger Lewis, Alan Phillips, Frans Bosch (all then of WRU), Paul Ackford (*The Times*), Rhodri Morgan, Huw Edwards (*Daily Mail*), Matthew Rhys (*The Times*), Leanne Wood, Lindsay Whittle, Jocelyn Davies, Rhuanedd Richards (all then of Plaid Cymru), George Monbiot (*The Guardian*), Valentine Low *(The Times)*, Prof T J Morgan, (Swansea University), John Osmond (Institute of Welsh Affairs*)*, Matthew Syed (*The Times)*, Niall Ferguson, Senior Fellow, Hoover Institution of Stanford University (*The Times)*, Report commissioned by Dyfed-Powys Drug Intervention Programme to study substance abuse amongst Poles in Carmarthenshire 2008/9.

Finally, I would like to thank the following for providing various photographs:
* My interview subjects for some of their personal photographs
* Alan Moss, photographer, for his photo of Côr Meibion Y Machlyd
* My wife Gill for her painting of St Illtyd's Church, Llantwit Major
* Skydive Hibaldstow's photo of Cledwyn's 65th birthday skydive
* Caerphilly County Borough Council for permission to show their photo of Blackwood's Chartist Bridge & Statue.

Peter Daniels
July 2017

What is Wales?

Not Yet a Nation

THE WELSH MIGHT feel they constitute a nation, but they have yet to form a nation state.

With the decline of the Roman Empire, around about 500AD, Wales was a land of many kingships and dynasties, but these were never unified into a single entity.

The difficulties were numerous. Geographically, the land of Wales is dominated by a central mountain core which makes travel difficult, especially between north and south. The earliest major highway for trade and commerce was in fact the Irish Sea. Yet we were ripe for invasion from the east, both down the valleys and along the coast. However, as Jon Gower points out in *The Story of Wales*, the landscape, and the decentralised nature of the Welsh, was also an advantage, and helped deny the Normans full control of the land. Whilst England was effectively subdued by the Normans in a mere four years, there were still parts of Wales that eluded Norman rule even after twenty-five years.

Economically, good agricultural land was small, scarce and scattered, and the custom of dividing estates equally between surviving male heirs (*gavelkind*) served to diminish the size of landholdings even further.

No urban tradition was established. In the twelfth century Giraldus Cambrensis (Gerald of Wales) wrote, 'the Welsh people do not live in towns.'

Yet there was still a great sense of community. J Geraint Jenkins observed in *Life and Traditions in Rural Wales* that 'in medieval Welsh society the law of civil obligation meant that at harvest time... cooperation was very widely practised, and the individual farmer considered it his duty to help his neighbour, knowing that this favour would be repaid when the need arose.'

He goes on to say, 'Strangers who visit parts of rural Wales are often impressed by the great deal of kindness, hospitality, and welcome they receive. This again is but a reflection of the tribal past and owes its origin to the keeping of an open house for those in need.

'Although in areas of dispersed settlement no village as such may be found, the very way of life and the whole social atmosphere... are such, that a kind of family feeling, an idea of common destiny... exists between each family and the whole locality. Rural Wales, the land of local cultures, supports a society as tribal in its organisation today as that of the early inhabitants described in the Welsh laws.

'The relative isolation... and the distribution of the homesteads... have tended to emphasise the individuality of character. When folk foregathered, it was not on the village green... or in the village tavern... as in England, but around the hearth of the individual farmstead' and in addition 'much of the informality of the hearth has been transferred to the services of the local places of worship and to concerts held in the parish halls... The latter still possess much of the informality of the traditional Welsh *Noson Lawen* (literally 'merry evening') which was once commonly conducted in the farm kitchen.'

Eventually, according to John Davies in *A History of Wales*, the Welsh king Hywel Dda (Hywel the Good) systemised the legal customs that had developed over the centuries. The emphasis was on reconciliation between kinship groups rather than keeping order through punishment. Key elements were mercy, common sense and respect for women and children. Many benefits of these laws were then unfortunately lost with the demise of Welsh independence under Edward I of England.

Edward took possession of the Principality during 1282 and

1283, and the Statute of Rhuddlan in 1284 introduced English common law, initially to just Gwynedd and Conwy in North Wales, and subsequently piecemeal throughout South Wales via the justices in Carmarthen and Cardigan.

The law of Wales was still permitted in relation to land, but not criminal offences. Historians have previously seen the provision of a strong royal law as Edward's greatest achievement, but this was based on the assumption that strict order is society's greatest glory, and the mistaken assumption, according to John Davies, that the law of Wales was primitive. In fact the law of the crown could be merciless, and people yearned for the tolerance of the law of Hywel.

The Normans, and later Edward I, built castles to subjugate the Welsh. Edward, one of the most formidable and effective of all English kings, spent £80,000 in the process. The building of such castles almost bankrupted the king, and it is ironic that in modern times they have become major focal points for the new Wales's main industry of tourism.

Around the castles were built garrison towns. Business and trade were required to be conducted within the town walls and many Welsh people had to hand over their lands to English settlers. With the growth of a monetary economy, taxes were also required paying for the first time in cash, causing much hardship to the local Welsh.

The urban structure replicated throughout all the towns of Wales was of an English gentry residing within the town walls and a Welsh peasantry inhabiting land outside the walls. For example, the outer Aberystwyth district of Trefechan roughly translates into English as 'township', very much perhaps in the manner of those that were to be found much later in apartheid South Africa. The analogy can also possibly be extended to reflect the living conditions in these 'townships', and the manner in which the Welsh or Welsh speakers were excluded from certain jobs.

There continued to be attempts by Welsh princes to unite Wales as a country, the most notable, in myth and in fact, being that of Owain Glyn Dŵr. Following the latter's revolt at the beginning of the fifteenth century, a series of penal statutes were passed, preventing Welshmen from owning land in England, and holding down any local position of authority in Wales. To quote Harold Carter, in his IWA (Institute of Welsh Affairs) publication *Against the Odds*, 'The identity of the Welsh was clearly recognised, even if only in the context of penalisation.'

Such was not the case with the other significant landmark of English rule, the Acts of Union of 1536 and 1542 introduced by the supposedly Welsh king, Henry VIII (although these were officially called the Laws in Wales Acts, they have been known as the Acts of Union since the early twentieth century). Whilst giving Welshmen the same rights as the English, these Acts stated that henceforth Wales would be 'incorporated united and annexed to' England. And anyone wishing to stand for public office had to do so through the medium of English. To again quote Harold Carter, 'This was not an outright ban on the use of Welsh but effectively limited the domains in which it could be used with the clear assumption of a gradual decay and ultimate disappearance.'

One can begin to understand the derivation of the Welsh disdain of financial ambition, and the disregard for the so-called *crach* of the upper classes. Historically, to succeed in life one had to speak English, preferably with an English accent; one had to become English instead of Welsh.

To continue with Harold Carter's theme, 'these enactments were manifestly directed at the total elimination not only of the Welsh laws that embodied so much of the Welsh way of life but also of all those customs and traditions which were distinctly Welsh, that is to destroy the culture and ethnic identity of the Welsh. To jump forward in time, it has become a cliché to quote the entry from the 1880 edition of the Encyclopaedia Britannica, "Wales, see England". It has aroused anger and scorn presumably because it was wrong and mistaken. But, in fact, it should arouse anger and scorn because it was manifestly true and correct since after the Act of Union Wales ceased to exist.'

Certainly in terms of the formation of political, economic and social institutions, the territorial integrity of Wales has continually been ignored, even up to the present day. Monmouthshire has always been treated as part of the Oxford section of the judicial circuit. Even in the 1960s the maps of the Ordnance Survey treated it as part of England. Monmouthshire rugby clubs are, as a consequence, permitted to be part of both the WRU and the RFU.

Welsh Water only covers part of Wales. Shrewsbury Postal Region serves the whole of mid Wales. The creation of television regions in the 1950s incorporated South Wales into Television Wales and West, and included North Wales as part of the Granada franchise covering north-west England. And we all know how impossible it is to travel from North to South Wales by either road or rail. The rail journey can only be achieved via a detour through Shrewsbury in England. Is it any wonder that North and South Walians don't understand each other? The northerners' word for us southerners, *hwntws*, translates as 'outsiders'.

And finally, Harold Carter even brings us a contemporary observation that 'when at the 2001 Census a question was put as to ethnic identity, the possible answer "Welsh" was excluded, replicating with surprising acumen the position taken by the *Encyclopaedia Britannica*.'

Mr Carter concludes: 'The question immediately arises as to how in fact the Welsh identity survived.'

The Act of Union drove a wedge between the peasantry (*y werin*) and the gentry, with the former preserving their own and separate culture, partly through sheer remoteness from the centres of power and, in the absence of institutions, via the language. At this stage in the history of Wales, language could be said to be synonymous with identity.

Ironically the 'vulgar Welsh tongue' was saved by the decision of the Elizabethans to make the Bible available in Welsh so that 'the Prince of Darkness might not altogether possess the Principality of Wales.' According to Harold Carter, the translation thus 'has nothing to do with the status of language but everything to do with saving of souls.' He quotes Glanmor Williams in the *Encyclopaedia of Wales*: 'The year in which English independence was preserved by the defeat of the Armada (1588) was also the year in which the linguistic and cultural integrity of Wales was saved by Morgan's Bible.'

The process of preservation was further assisted by the circulating schools of Griffith Jones, Vicar of Llanddowror in Carmarthenshire, which involved itinerant teachers staying at given locations for three month spells to teach reading, and thus increase the accessibility of the Bible. David Williams in *A History of Modern Wales* argues that Griffith Jones 'helped to make the Welsh a literate nation.'

Then slowly through the eighteenth century, Calvinistic Methodism took root in Wales. Described by Jon Gower in *The Story of Wales* as 'a religion of the people... with a strong sense of moral self-discipline that seemed to chime with the experience of the Welsh, who liked to work hard and pray hard.' Through the fire and brimstone preaching of ministers such as Howell Harris and Daniel Rowland, and the singing of the many hymns of William Williams Pantycelyn (such as *Bread of Heaven*) the Methodist movement helped to create a much greater sense of self-awareness amongst the Welsh people. Harold Carter argues that, deprived of any knowledge of Welsh history, the story of Israel provided a parallel and surrogate through which the identity of any small country could be forged.

There was also a growing secular Welsh self-consciousness during the period of the late Renaissance leading into the Age of Enlightenment, fostered by books, eisteddfodau and debating societies. Writes Jon Gower: 'this was a time when newspapers were the vehicles of political education, but it was also a period that saw a burgeoning in book production. In the 1760s there were some 230 books in Welsh; 30 years later there were nearly 500 such tomes. Bodies such as the Cowbridge Book Society busily distributed the latest volumes, whilst a bookseller in Merthyr took weekly consignments to London.

When he left college, all he wanted to do was race cars, and thought the best way to achieve this was to work in the motor trade. He ended up selling Mercedes in Cardiff, and with the reasonable amount of commission was able to buy and race a car, although on reflection says he couldn't really afford it.

After five fruitless years of pursuing his passion, he decided he should take a more serious approach to life, and in 1970 joined Cooper Brothers in Cardiff to train as an accountant.

To be successful in the company meant a posting at some stage to London. On qualification he was persuaded to transfer temporarily to the London office. From there events took over and apart from a two-year posting to Nassau, in the Bahamas, he spent the rest of his career in the London office of Coopers (which subsequently became PricewaterhouseCoopers).

His work at PwC was principally in the area of financial investigations, including mergers and acquisitions, corporate reconstructions and flotations. During the 1980s and 1990s he was extensively involved in the UK Government privatisation programme and was, among other things, responsible for the accounting input for the Welsh operations of British Steel and South Wales Electricity.

Roger didn't return to live in Wales until the mid-nineties. His eldest son was struggling in school in Ascot and whilst watching the school play Monmouth at rugby, it occurred to him and his wife that here was a schooling option for the two boys. They went to have a look at Monmouth School, and were impressed, not only by its academic record but by the general atmosphere, including the sports facilities. Roger also liked the idea of exposing the boys to a more Welsh and less London-centric culture.

So the family moved back to Monmouthshire for the boys to attend the school, whilst Roger lived from Monday to Friday in a flat in the City of London. They now consider it the best move they have ever made. The children were very happy and did well in school, and Roger has now moved down full time in retirement, whilst one of the sons has taken over the residency of the family flat to work in London.

Roger had a very happy childhood in Newport. There wasn't a lot of Welshness, and he hardly ever heard the language spoken. But he has always felt Welsh and admits that he has always assumed he would return. The family regularly visited his mother, and late on a Friday night crossing the Severn Bridge he always insisted that they all sing *Sosban Fach*, even if he had to wake up the two boys for them to join in.

The boys in their turn see themselves as 100% Welsh, with, according to Roger, no coercion, and loved being in school in Wales. They were Welshmen who had never before lived in Wales. They were earlier also often to be seen with Roger at London Welsh.

He finds Monmouthshire people mostly regard themselves as Welsh, but on their own terms. They don't want the language shoved down their throats, but they are happy to have their kids learn Welsh.

He has attempted and failed to learn the language, but his house contains all the evidence of Welshness. Books on Wales and Welsh poetry. Paintings of the local area painted personally for him by local artists, and a love of rugby and choral music, even if he can't sing a note. And on the wall of the London flat hangs a variant of that famous old verse:

To be born Welsh is to be born privileged
Not with a silver spoon in your mouth,
But with music in your heart
And poetry in your soul.

His workplace, Cooper Brothers, mainly took people's backgrounds for granted, as employees came from all over the UK and overseas. Yet your typical Coopers person was public school and Oxbridge educated who always presumed they would become an accountant and do well.

So in this context, they looked at Roger as a bit of an oddity, a 'country bumpkin'. He found it strange he was known to be Welsh, as he doesn't have a pronounced Welsh accent, but he must have spoken up, particularly extolling the strength of Welsh rugby to well-known rugby players such as Paul Wallace, also employed by the firm. Love of rugby has always been a great Welsh identifier.

And in the Bahamas he soon looked up the Welsh members of staff.

Famous rugby player Delme Thomas writes in his autobiography of how, on Lions tours, ex-pat Welshmen always sought out the Welsh players in the touring party, far more than the equivalent English, Irish or Scottish exiles went in search of their home-grown players.

Roger's wife, Margaret, was born in Slough, daughter of a Welsh father and a Scottish mother. After qualifying as a nurse she immediately sought work overseas, mainly in Australia, but also South Africa. She sees herself as English, but as a much-travelled woman of the world, she doesn't see it as particularly relevant.

Roger met her on one of her fleeting visits from Australia. He also visited her in South Africa. Then when she was finally coming home, she wrote to him, quoting her flight number, saying it would be nice to see him. He duly picked her up from the airport on the day before Christmas Eve and drove her to her parents' place in Norfolk. By then it was quite late, so Roger had to stay the night. Margaret's Dad, being Welsh, immediately suggested going down the pub. After a heavy session, Roger retired to bed, to discover the following morning that he seemed to be engaged. They were married on 2nd January; it was the first time Margaret had met Roger's parents.

Margaret has now lived in Wales for almost twenty years. She likes it, the house, and friendships that would never have happened in Teddington or Virginia Water.

In Teddington, everybody worked for Thames Television. To quote Roger, 'They were a strange lot of people, throwing themselves off the top of houses, and going stark naked in the middle of the night.' In their little cul de sac of around twelve houses, at the end of four years, they were the only couple still left married.

Virginia Water was particularly toffee-nosed, and people were too busy at work to make any strong friendships.

Roger and Margaret now live way out in the country, two miles down a single track lane, off the Monmouth to Abergavenny road. They find Monmouthshire people far more down to earth, farmers and schoolteachers, ordinary people, with no side to them. They meet in the pub and get to know each other, without being too intrusive. Living in an isolated area, they learn to look out for each other, especially when away from their properties, doing things without even being asked. And Roger and Margaret have as a result developed really strong and lasting friendships.

One doesn't notice precisely when the border is crossed into Herefordshire, but according to Roger, thereafter one does spot the difference. Herefordshire is full of gastro pubs; whilst many in Monmouth are closing down. And in Monmouthshire one notices the bilingual road signs, Welsh being spoken in shops, conversations about rugby as opposed to soccer, and an orientation towards Cardiff as opposed to London.

Almost by accident Roger has found himself involved in things Welsh. At a chance meeting with a former colleague in Cardiff, it was suggested to Roger that he might like to get involved in the administrative side of our alma mater, Aberystwyth University. He has thus been an unpaid member of the governing council and various operating committees since 2003, as well as being a director of one of the university's spin-off companies.

He has also acted as treasurer for the Bridges Community Centre, a substantial independent charity based in Monmouth, and remains involved in all its financial matters.

His Aberystwyth activities require attendance at meetings three or four times a month, each of which means spending a day or two in Aberystwyth, only reached by a 100-mile, two-and-a-half hour journey cross country from Monmouth.

The meetings are often held in Welsh, so learning the language would be of benefit. But his one abortive attempt was abandoned, the final straw being the laughter which his efforts induced amongst some of his friends.

His efforts for the university have resulted in him meeting many Welsh politicians. Their lack of understanding of Aberystwyth's needs and their lack of appreciation of how little industry exists in Mid Wales only supports his views that Wales hasn't been well served by either Cardiff's Assembly or Westminster. Education ministers, he feels, are doing things for personal and political reasons, not for what's good in the long term for Wales.

Roger, like the majority of my returning exiles, is not impressed by developments in Cardiff Bay. But I feel this could be a function of too little as opposed to too much power, and let us hope such feelings do not discourage us from the very necessary loosening of our ties with Westminster's 'English' Parliament. Otherwise we will lose the opportunity to govern ourselves, both to put Wales first for once, and to see if our very powerful sense of community cannot be utilised to create a far more democratic, less materialistic overall society and nationhood.

Hiraeth

EXILES OF ALL nationalities, having ventured afield to earn their fortune or broaden their horizons, often have a desire to return home, to an environment and community with which they more clearly identify. There are Welsh exiles, however, who have a deeper longing (*hiraeth*), not just for the people and places of their upbringing, but for a more fundamental reunion with the language, music and human values that are the essence of the Welsh character and culture.

Retirement may have given them the opportunity to achieve this reunion, or perhaps the right job prospect has fortunately come their way at the right time.

They may, however, find that with the greater mobilisation and globalisation of this world, their homeland and its residents have changed, and they therefore recognise a need to involve themselves more actively in the community to ensure that the values and customs they hold dear are maintained and preserved for the future.

Huw Jones

Huw Jones was born in Llangyfelach on the outskirts of Swansea. His father was a fitter and turner at the Trostre tinplate works in Llanelli, his mother a primary school teacher until her marriage.

The village and family were Welsh-speaking. The family were worshippers at a Welsh Methodist Chapel, and Huw's mother sang at local eisteddfodau.

Prior to attending school, Huw's first language had been Welsh, but his education was mainly through the medium of English. So the family at home began to speak a mixture of the two languages, and over time Huw and his younger sister would begin to answer in English questions asked of them in Welsh. The family would eventually focus more on English as their main language.

As a child I had seldom encountered such Welsh-speaking families in the centre of Llanelli, and I had always assumed that Swansea was even more anglicised. But rugby player Mervyn Davies, now sadly deceased, spoke similarly of his upbringing in west Swansea, and I'm sure all the Welsh speakers attending Llanelli Grammar School who hailed from the villages of rural Carmarthenshire could tell a similar tale. And the scenario is not that dissimilar to Welsh-speaking families I have encountered in exile in England.

Yet in retirement back in Wales, Huw now actually finds himself speaking more Welsh with his contemporaries, at meetings of the University of the Third Age, and at the bilingual golf club, than he did in his childhood, even though the area probably contains fewer Welsh speakers in general. And his wife, Eira, is taking Welsh lessons to remind herself of her forgotten childhood Welsh. Parents on both sides were Welsh speakers, and there exists a strong desire to preserve the language.

But shopping in Llanelli is conducted in English, and Huw has not encouraged his son and daughter, brought up in England, to speak Welsh. Although true to form, Wales are supported at sport, his son has Principality Stadium debentures, and his grandson has both Wales and Ospreys kits. It is always a matter of debate whether the language or the rugby team has had the biggest influence on the preservation of our Welsh identity.

Huw studied at Gowerton Grammar School, subsequently accepting a place at the London School of Economics. As a student in London, he didn't become involved in London Welsh circles. In fact it continues to be one of the overriding challenges of the London Welsh Centre in Gray's Inn Road to increase the level of interaction between the centre and the Welsh student population of the metropolis.

Huw's social activities mainly centred on sport, especially football, and he played most weekends for the LSE First XI, as well as occasionally for a team brought together by sports journalist Brian Glanville.

Huw then returned to the University of Swansea to obtain a teaching diploma, before winning a scholarship to undertake research for the university's geography department into the population movement of the Welsh in the USA. Completion of his thesis would have involved being based in the States, a step too far for home-loving Huw. He didn't want the upheaval: he was happy with his life, particularly his love of sport. Perhaps, he feels, he wasn't ambitious enough.

Whilst at Swansea he also met his future wife Eira, at a dance hall in Mumbles. And after six years in university and with the prospect of getting married, he felt he ought to get a 'proper' job. Despite applying locally, the first post he was offered was at a Further Education College in Essex. After two years there he landed a more senior position at Birmingham's College of Commerce, an institution which offered external degrees. Huw spent the rest of his career at the same college, although its name changed several times over the period, to Polytechnic, then to the University of Central England, and it is now the Birmingham City University. Huw's involvement also switched from the geography department to being a senior lecturer in the town-planning department. He retired at 61 in the year 2000.

Working in the Midlands, Huw initially bought a house in Polesworth, near Atherstone, and from there, after six years, the family relocated to Sutton Coldfield.

Much of Huw's social life still centred on sport. After informing the Essex college on his CV that he had an interest in cricket, the captain of the staff cricket team called at his house on the very day he moved in to ask if he could turn out for the team the following day. The school term had still to begin.

During his two years in Essex, Huw also played football for Coggeshall Town, in the Essex and Suffolk Border League.

Whilst in Sutton Coldfield the focus turned to tennis, with Huw becoming chairman of the local tennis club.

Huw hasn't followed the religious beliefs typical of previous generations in the Wales of the early part of the twentieth century. As a child he would attend chapel three times every Sunday, but he became more rebellious and less interested in religion in his teens. He has however maintained his left-wing political convictions, and whilst not being highly active in the Labour Party, he did canvass for them during his time in the Midlands.

Having a socialist bent meant that Huw was obviously pro comprehensive schools, but, as discussed earlier, such a system has not necessarily been sensibly introduced in all areas. In the Midlands, grammar schools still exist, and these tend to cream off the best talent in terms of both staff and pupils. And Huw was not about to disadvantage his kids for the sake of his principles. A circumstance with which I am only too familiar.

Huw has made a success of his career in education, and has led a very pro-active social life. He has mixed well, not confining himself to seeking out fellow Welsh people, although the family of his wife's cousin also lived for some years in the Midlands, even being founder members of the Birmingham Welsh Rugby Club.

But throughout all these years there was no sense of belonging to Sutton Coldfield society. As Huw puts it, 'you always felt to some extent an outsider', especially when the family first moved into the area.

They lived in a very 'middle-class' road, and the differences became obvious when you talked to people about various topics, particularly about their deep-down political roots.

Huw was not averse to having the 'mickey' taken out of his Welsh identity, particularly his accent. The Birmingham accent would be similarly treated in Wales. But there was a sense, in both his academic workplace and the tennis club, that any regional accent, Welsh or otherwise, was frowned upon, as if it were a sign of a lower intelligence. Huw had even wondered on occasions whether your accent actually reduced your chances of promotion. And he was not alone amongst my sample of exiles in knowing at least one other exile who had an inflated sense of their own importance, severely anglicising their Welsh accent in an attempt to appear superior, or at least, less inferior.

And whilst he had many English acquaintances whose friendship he truly valued, and thought that Midlanders were in fact more akin to Welsh people than those in the South East, he feels that as a nation the English have difficulty in avoiding the sense of superiority with which they appear to have been born.

Wales was more egalitarian, where any elitism was quickly knocked out of you.

He also sees the Welsh as more passionate and emotional, and thus, more welcoming, open to outsiders, contrary to some English people's views about the cold reception they may have received, particularly in North Wales.

So when retirement beckoned, and with the kids having fled the nest to Bristol and Reading, where would Huw and Eira want to end their days? There was only one place: 'back home'.

West Wales provided them with a much greater sense of belonging. This sense was obviously encouraged by the fact that much of Huw's long college holidays had been spent with relatives in Swansea and Pontarddulais. Huw's Welsh accent was always said to be a few shades broader when he returned to college each autumn. In addition, both sets of parents, along with a sister and numerous cousins, still lived in the area when Huw and Eira returned there.

But the sense of belonging was broader than just family. Huw and Eira felt more comfortable with people in general. Their sense of humour was similar, along with their working-class values, respecting people for what they were, not making judgements and not seeing anyone as better than anyone else.

Huw describes Pontarddulais society as more 'cosmopolitan' – not, I think, in the sense that there is more variety, but that there are fewer distinctions of class, with people of all creeds and persuasions being made welcome.

In more specific terms, Huw talks about people passing the

time of day in the street far more frequently. In Sutton Coldfield this would only cause passersby to give you strange looks.

And people are more caring, although Huw does add that this might be a function of a rural versus urban culture rather than the difference between the Welsh and the English. He quotes the staff of an industrial unit close to his home coming out to a nearby field to help a lady who had collapsed while walking her dog. They took the lady to hospital, and the manager continued to make enquiries afterwards about her state of health.

When a lady was similarly affected in Huw's street in Sutton Coldfield, no one came to her rescue, and Huw's offer of help was rather reluctantly accepted by the lady, who too strongly valued her privacy. Huw, in fact, did end up taking her to hospital.

We also keep forgetting how nice a physical environment is on offer in West Wales, especially now the mines and steelworks have disappeared. Within easy reach of Huw's home are both an attractive coastline and majestic mountains. Huw and Eira go on many an outing, and only the day before we met, they had spent a pleasant day shopping for antiques in the increasingly smart town of Llandeilo, still managing to keep the supermarkets at bay.

And finally, there is the Welsh language and all the culture that goes with it. Huw and Eira are not eisteddfodau attendees, but regular viewers via S4C.

Living in England I am constantly conscious of the extreme efforts I feel I have to make to connect with any Welsh news, sport or culture. I asked Huw whether living in Wales he felt equally disadvantaged.

Like most returning exiles I have encountered, media wasn't a big issue for Huw. If you lived in Wales you could always buy the *Western Mail*, and it was also now available online. The world has changed with the internet.

BBC Wales also has lots of Welsh sport, and even the *Sunday Times* has a Welsh rugby writer in Stephen Jones. Birmingham papers on the other hand didn't even feature rugby, leave alone Welsh rugby. Huw also felt that Swansea City FC hadn't received the attention it deserved prior to the quality of the team's football forcing more recognition.

I have tried to explore the roots of my greater antagonism towards the 'British' media in comparison to the views held by these residents of Wales. My default TV channel is BBC London whereas those in Wales tune in to a BBC which features a Wales logo. They are made immediately aware of programmes specifically concerned with Wales whereas I have to go in search via the television guide, and BBC Wales does actually probably feature more Welsh sport than English channels devote to English sport.

But my mindset is that I am watching English television, and attention given to Wales is minimal. In Wales they feel coverage of Welsh matters is adequate, and for the rest they are tuning into British programming in which Welsh people play a part. They feel a part of the UK. I feel a Welsh exile in England.

Huw's attitudes towards politics however do accord more closely to my own. He feels that historically Wales has been 'hard done by', and that currently Wales is not getting 'a fair crack of the whip' from a rigged Barnett Formula.

He is therefore a firm believer in the Welsh Assembly, that as a mature society we should have a say in running our own affairs, and in fact feels that England has been looking over its shoulder at some of things we are doing right in Wales, compared to its original attitude of 'How dare they do it differently?'

But he does not consider the Assembly to be perfect by any means. There are question marks about the quality of the people and there is a need for far greater tax-raising powers to enable many of the initiatives to reach fruition.

Huw does not think that full independence is impossible. He has had dealings with the Maltese government and seen how such a small nation, with a population of about 360,000, can still successfully govern itself. But he probably favours a UK federal system, along the lines of the USA, with a certain level of independence for each state, without each individual entity being encumbered by all the broader responsibilities of nationhood, such as defence. Thus avoiding the question, asked by *Dragon's Eye* presenter David Williams of Plaid candidate Bethan Jenkins, 'How many aircraft carriers would an independent Wales have?'

Huw however believes that it is important to encourage the Welsh language, and views as a good sign the growth of Welsh schools and Welsh in schools. He likes the concept of bilingualism, jokingly adding that he doesn't want to cut out English completely.

But the Pontarddulais of today is very different from his youth, with the rapid growth of new housing to accommodate both retired couples, often English, and younger commuters working in Swansea. Previously part of Wales's 'industrial backbone', the village has now become a 'dormitory settlement', a suburb of Swansea, with the city also being the main focus of entertainment.

Huw recognises the need to involve people more in the local community, and is doing his own bit for the cause. He has been secretary and, until recently, chairman of the local U3A (University of the Third Age), even being happy to hold meetings in the village's Conservative Club. The club have in fact been extremely hospitable hosts.

Huw is also a trustee of the Pontarddulais Village Partnership which undertakes useful community work such as sponsoring kids' play schemes, renovating a local historic churchyard, as well as establishing a credit union to assist non-bank account holders amongst the unemployed, helping them avoid loan sharks in their search for capital. Huw, along with his wife Eira, was involved with a similar but more advanced scheme in Birmingham. There is also an educational centre which helps develop skill sets such as the writing of CVs.

The overall focus is on employment, regeneration and the preservation of the village's community spirit.

Richard Davies

I first met Richard in the 1970s on the courts of the Cambrian Lawn Tennis Club in the North-London suburb of Cricklewood. He and his brother, Lod, were also members of the London Welsh Centre in Gray's Inn Road, of which Lod was still a member until his untimely death in the summer of 2015.

The family hailed originally from Ceredigion, although at the time of Richard's birth, his parents ran a dairy and bottling plant in Clerkenwell in the City of London.

Richard's elder brother and sister were in fact born in London, but his mother when pregnant with Richard left London during the Blitz and Richard was actually born prematurely in Aberystwyth in 1941.

Both he and his siblings were evacuated to Aberystwyth, the brother and sister living with a strict aunt, whilst Richard stayed on the farm with his grandparents and uncles. He hardly knew his parents for the first few years of his life. Welsh was also the only language spoken on the farm, and Richard even understood Italian more than English, acquired through speaking to the prisoners of war set to work on the farm.

Richard moved to London when he was five, still unable to converse in English, and his entry into infant school was delayed whilst he was told to go home and speak only English for half a term before he would be allowed back to school.

The final insult, which prompted a rapid improvement in his English, came at the age of nine, when he was told by a teacher in front of the whole class that he could only play a soldier, a non-speaking part, in the school play, because he still couldn't read. This prompted special tuition, plus the reading of lots of books, the result of which saw Richard, at the age of eleven, passing the entrance exam to the City of London independent boys' school.

After leaving school, Richard worked briefly for his father, a typical London Welsh dairyman with two shops which also sold groceries and light refreshments. But the likes of Tesco wiped out the bulk of their milk business, and Richard instead helped develop a supply business to twenty-one Welsh-owned shops in and around the City, buying in bulk and delivering to them. On one occasion he visited Barclays Bank to query something on the accounts, was offered a job interview, and spent the rest of his working life with the bank.

He started as a junior in Silver Town, a public schoolboy dumped right in the middle of the East End, and then proceeded to work across twenty-six different branches, in branch, marketing and training managerships, and ended his career in a pivotal role as the manager responsible for arranging branch closures and mergers. This didn't make him particularly popular, and led to him being largely snubbed at the next leaving party. He had told his wife he would be home late, but found himself leaving the party after one quick pint.

He also encountered at the party the wife of one of the managers he had made redundant. She had presumed six months after the redundancy that her husband was still working, as such was his shame that he still adopted the pretence of catching the train for work every morning.

Richard was on one, occasion, however able to put his Welshness to good account. When he had staffing problems in Finsbury Park, where there were eleven different nationalities working on site, he was able to get the staff on his side by claiming that he was a Welshman who didn't like the English either. The branch manager who had caused the unrest had been particularly narrow-minded and racist, objecting to black members of staff actually serving at the counter.

Richard had initially been keen on a transfer to South Wales, but the bank was short staffed in the London area and insisted on him staying on in the metropolis.

It was in London at the Cambrian Lawn Tennis Club that Richard also met his future wife, Mary. Her family had lived in Penybont, near Llandrindod Wells in Powys, for more than 200 years, but by now her parents had moved to London, apart from the duration of the Second World War during which her mother had been evacuated to the old family home in Powys. Her mum had been a teacher and her dad a scientist with Cable and Wireless.

Richard got married in 1966, and would describe his life in London as essentially British.

He played rugby for Barclays Bank and set up a midweek team of employees.

He did however study Welsh, and RI in Welsh, for O-level, and kept his language fresh through occasional visits to Jewin Chapel, lessons at Gray's Inn Road and conversations with Welsh-speaking members of the Cambrian Lawn Tennis Club. Coming from Powys, Mary was a non-Welsh speaker, although fluent in French and German.

They had contemplated sending their two girls to the Welsh school in Willesden Green, but they only had the one car which was needed for Richard's work, and Mary was adamant that the girls should be educated more locally, with local friends, after her own experience of boarding school.

The girls, having initially considered themselves Welsh but now living in Stamford and Bristol, one with a Welsh/Irish husband with some Jewish antecedents, would probably describe themselves as British with Welsh connections. Although, as seems to be the norm amongst offspring of Welsh exiles, they still support the Welsh rugby team.

And both Richard and Mary always knew they would return to Wales in retirement. Both were born in Wales. Mary's heart was always in Penybont, and Richard also had a *hiraeth* for family and friends, spending many holidays and weekends in West Wales.

As he puts it, 'the draw was, I'm Welsh, and I wanted to be in Wales.' Psychologically and emotionally, he wanted to live in Wales. 'I'm not English, I am Welsh; I have a democratic right to be Welsh. I choose to call myself Welsh and not British, all the time.'

For the move 'back home' they reviewed the three options of Swansea, Aberystwyth and Penybont, near Llandrindod. Mary felt that Aberystwyth would prove to be too Welsh-speaking, so they chose Mary's birthplace of Penybont, which also happened to be more convenient for their two girls in London. As luck would have it, both had moved away from London within two years of Richard and Mary settling in Powys.

Richard recently returned to London for a visit, staying with Welsh hoteliers Royden and Gwen Rees in Gower Street. He confessed to no longer feeling much at home in the noisy urban scene that is London, appalled by the tasteless commercialism evident in, for example, what once must have been the elegant sweep of old Regent Street. Although, standing in the hotel's gorgeous walled garden, free from the noise of traffic, he did have second thoughts about whether he could live in London.

Richard however has always possessed a latent desire to have 'a bit of a farm'. And in Powys, Richard and Mary have a share, with Mary's brother, of a sixteen-acre smallholding adjacent to the old family home.

From his early childhood days Richard had retained a knowledge of, and a sympathy for, farming, so he has quite quickly grasped the fundamentals of farm management. He could in addition turn for advice to his farming cousin. Also, in London, both his daughters had ridden horses, and he had long had the desire to breed his own.

The alternative to farming would have been working in some capacity with the Welsh Development Agency, which would certainly have been his best option if they had moved to Swansea. His efforts to obtain such a position in Powys however failed in the face of a certain amount of what he regarded as local cronyism.

So how Welsh have Richard and Mary found Powys, non-Welsh speaking and very close to the English border?

Richard doesn't describe Llandrindod and Penybont as a Welsh community, but as a community in Wales. He feels there are three basic strands to the population: Welsh locals, or people with a long local history who are returning to their childhood environs; English immigrants, both retired couples and those being dumped in social housing by authorities in the English Midlands, and Eastern European immigrants.

In addition, Llandrindod is 95% white.

Those of Welsh origin probably only now represent around 50% of the population, and retired English couples, whilst having a love of the area, still see it as being governed by Westminster. And whilst becoming involved in societies such as the U3A and the Pensioners' Club, most have no interest in the Historical Society or the Radnorshire Society. The last named also, whilst being fervently Welsh, has only a few Welsh speakers.

Richard has always seen himself as a 'pink Tory'. But on his return to Wales he has seen the work done by the Lib Dems in the regeneration of Powys, and recognises the need for a Welsh Assembly with more freedom to interpret Westminster's guidelines along with more tax-raising powers. Wales needs to be seen more as an entity in its own right, both in terms of the need to preserve Welsh culture and language, and to meet the requirements of a rural economy which tends to be neglected by the politicians of the South East who have no feeling for, nor knowledge of, anything outside their own environment. He sees the South East as reaping the benefits of absolutely everything.

Richard is not a nationalist, believing we don't have the income to survive, and he even is a supporter of royalty (well, at least of the Queen, drawing the line at the philandering of Prince Charles). But he is still 'a Welshman who is proud of being a Welshman.' He sees us as warm hearted, emotional, with a sense of both humour and communality. He is emotional about wanting to live in Wales, and finds it comforting to be in Wales, to be able to shout across the street and speak to someone in Welsh.

He doesn't go around waving a Welsh flag, but he does put one up outside the house when Wales are playing rugby, and leaves it up when we win.

And both he and Mary have contributed greatly to the local community, including many activities relating to their Welshness.

Richard is treasurer of the Radnorshire Society, which is producing a calendar of local views, hopefully with bilingual commentary. He is also a member of the sinister-sounding movement *Cymdeithas y Ddraig Goch* (Society of the Red Dragon), which is Llandrindod's Welsh Society. And he spoke on behalf of the local community council in opposition to certain excessive housing development programmes.

Both Richard and Mary are members of the local U3A, and Mary runs its history group.

They support things Welsh such as the Royal Welsh Show, of which they are members, and local school eisteddfodau.

Richard is also a member of the local Rotary Club, now unfortunately on the verge of extinction. I have always seen the Rotary as having typical English associations, an impression generated perhaps by the lack of historical association between Wales and business in general, conducted as it was in English and mainly by Englishmen.

But the Rotary in fact is a North-American creation which sees itself as an international service organisation designed to bring together business and professional leaders to provide humanitarian services, encourage ethical standards and help build goodwill and peace in the world. Its motto of 'Service above self' is not radically different from the feelings generated by the community spirit that exists in Wales. Richard even took an HGV driving test to be able to deliver a lorry load of medicines and Christmas presents to those fighting in Bosnia.

The Eastern-European immigrants Richard sees as hard working, prepared to take on unwanted tasks. For example, during the foot-and-mouth epidemic, three-quarters of the slaughterhouse staff were Polish. And there are some immigrant families enthusiastically encouraging their offspring to develop their Welsh language skills, including competing in the Urdd Eisteddfod.

What of the next generation? The nearest Welsh-language school is in fact in Builth Wells, but the local school concert was delivered half in Welsh, even though the pupils were Welsh learners rather than Welsh speakers.

So there is still hope? *Yma o hyd*.

Do not the South Wales Valleys, where immigration was greatest at the turn of the last century, now, according to the latest census, have the highest percentage of population who regard themselves as Welsh?

And the new worlds of the Americas and Australasia are also living proof of immigrants warmly adopting the flag of their new countries. They are also unfortunately examples of the wholesale destruction of indigenous populations, and over the centuries it could be claimed that Wales has been nothing more than a colony of England in its own lands.

So there is also still much work to be done.

Peter Williams

And finally we have Peter Williams, who is living proof that having a sense of *hiraeth* for the values and character of Welshness is not dependent on being a Welsh-speaker. Like me, he has tried and failed to master the language, and even throws into question the myth of Wales as the Land of Song, given his claim that he can't sing to save his life.

His background, in fact, is a close parallel to my own. He was born in hospital in Swansea but raised in Llanelli's Swiss Valley a few doors up from my Aunty Etta, who was friendly with his mother. He is the only son of a fluent Welsh-speaking father, from Pottery Street, whilst his non-Welsh speaking mother was born, like my own mother, in the Llanelli district of Seaside – in her case in Glanmor Road, where her parents owned a small bakery and grocer shop. Peter's maternal grandfather's family hailed originally from Hay on Wye on the English border, now world famous for its annual book festival.

In such similar circumstances to my own, and many other homes in central Llanelli in the 1950s and 1960s, Welsh was only spoken by the one parent, the language thus unfortunately being lost to the new generation.

But Peter has grown up to adore Llanelli, its people, its scenery, its history. As he emotionally expresses it, 'There must be a God, as otherwise there wouldn't be a Llanelli.'

But his real pride and joy are the Scarlets. Brought up like me on a diet of rugby and weekly visits to Stradey Park, he is the ultimate supporter. He is these days the first in the queue to personally collect his season ticket (no purchasing on the internet for Peter), and his current dog is even called Scarlet the Second.

It is in fact questionable as to whether his *hiraeth* actually extends beyond Llanelli, as he at the same time very publicly disapproves of the Ospreys, Pontypridd, and anything east of the Loughor bridge. But he is very much also a supporter of the national team, claiming recently that he has actually attended as many as seventy-eight of Wales's away matches over the years.

After living for twenty-nine years away from Wales, he has returned in retirement to still make his contribution to the local culture. He is the treasurer of the Scarlets feeder club, Llanelli RFC, also treasurer of the Glanmor and Tyisha History Group, and a committee member of the Llanelli Community Heritage Group. He has a particular fondness for Seaside and the stories surrounding his family's bakery in Glanmor Road.

He is well aware of how Llanelli has changed, how the planners have almost obliterated the old town centre, and the current problems associated with drugs and with large-scale immigration. But he still loves the friendliness of the people and almost likes the fact that most are busybodies, wanting to know everyone's business.

He also recognises the need for all elements of society to integrate newcomers into their midst. His cousin is managing director of the SaveEasy Credit Union which offers financial help to all Llanelli residents, with Peter acting as its treasurer. He is also treasurer of the Polish Welsh Association. He feels that the local population should be more prepared to welcome the Poles who are happy to do a lot of the jobs that locals won't undertake, and equally he feels that the Poles should probably not keep to themselves so much.

For the older immigrants it is partly a function of language. On a recent Polish Welsh Association excursion, a son's presence was required to help translate conversations for his father.

This reminds me that we Welsh ourselves have historically to some extent been treated as immigrants in our own country, and I recall a not dissimilar situation of a young lad attending the 1962 National Eisteddfod with his grandfather, to help the old man when English was required to be spoken.

As far as drugs are concerned, Peter feels they are not as big a problem in the area as some people like to think. Llanelli is no worse than other towns, and the *Llanelli Star*, like all newspapers, has a tendency to inflate such issues. I'm not sure, however, that Peter is happy to walk down that den of iniquity, Station Road, late on a Saturday evening.

He has been able to assist in local matters as a consequence of his degree in business administration and accountancy acquired from UWIST in Cardiff. My sample of exiles does seem full of accountants.

But in the late 1970s and early 1980s work was difficult to come by in Wales. Peter is still of the opinion that Llanelli and Wales had the life kicked out of them by Maggie Thatcher's government. So his first job was as a graduate trainee for Scottish and Newcastle Brewery in Edinburgh. He worked on their internal audit, which involved travelling the country in five-star luxury; a great life for a young man in his twenties.

As he said goodbye to his mother on Llanelli station back in September 1981 he loudly proclaimed that 'one day, I'll be back', little realising it wouldn't happen for twenty-nine years, with his parents passed away and Peter in his fifties.

He loved Edinburgh and the Scottish people, and still visits friends there every two years when the Welsh rugby team are in town. But it was too far from home, especially with his then girlfriend living in Cardiff. However, his search for work didn't lead him home, but instead to Bracknell and International

Stores – later, after his departure, to become part of the Gateway supermarket group.

It was in south-east England that he met his wife Sandra, and they lived in Ascot for many years until his return to Llanelli.

Ascot is a lovely area, but everyone is in a rush, with no time to talk. And it takes so long to get anywhere. Peter's last position before early retirement was for a company in Chertsey, but for much of his career he was self-employed, operating under the banner of Red Dragon Accounting Ltd – usually working on contracts across London and the South East, avoiding if possible the slog of commuting into central London.

Peter and Sandra lived in a cul-de-sac. People rarely had the time or inclination to indulge in pleasantries, so they only probably spoke to four other houses on the estate. Although their immediate neighbours were still there for you in times of emergency.

Sandra was brought up in Shepperton, which as a child she knew as a pleasant, friendly village. She now sees it as a nondescript commuter town. Isn't it strange how many of the wives of our various Welsh exiles have maintained little affection for their own place of birth, but are happy to relocate to the environment of Wales?

Through Peter, Sandra has had plenty of time to get to know many Scarlets supporters on their frequent visits to Llanelli before relocating permanently, and she speaks positively of their friendliness. I wouldn't be surprised if Peter and Sandra made it down to most of Scarlets' home games, not forgetting that Peter also had to keep an eye on his ailing parents.

As an only child, he inherited the family home in Swiss Valley, and he returned here on retirement. Initially Sandra stayed in Ascot for her working week, only coming down to Llanelli at weekends, but she now works from home in Wales, and even her mother has moved down to live around the corner. Her new neighbours all sent her cards to welcome her, even before they had met. To quote Peter, 'It's Wales, what's not to like about it?'

As one might expect, Peter is a socialist, but he is fairly disenchanted with all recent governments and the National Assembly. He feels the latter is 'useless' and is also aware that its lack of power is due in no small measure to the Labour government that created it.

He would be happy to be governed from Westminster, but is conscious that these days it is totally London-centric. So he feels that Wales needs more recognition, but his answer is federalism, not nationalism. He claims that Wales can't survive on its own. And he is happy to be part of Britain. 'British by birth, Welsh by the grace of God.'

In the last analysis, national politics are not that important to Peter. To quote, yet again, travel writer Jan Morris, 'the Welsh have seldom suffered from national ambition, only national grievance.'

For Peter, living is about people, not politics. And in this respect, Wales is still 'the best country in the world'.

But perhaps these people also have to be Scarlets supporters. Peter, in direct opposition to Her Majesty (he is obviously a Republican), posts a Christmas message every year from his dog Scarlet the Second. In the last such message, Scarlet pens the wish for 'peace all over the world, except at the Liberty Stadium' (home of the Ospreys).

Working for Wales

THE LAST SECTION concerned itself with people who on their return to Wales in retirement were able to contribute to local and Welsh society and culture. But there are also exiles who were motivated, or had the opportunity, to return to Wales earlier in their lives to continue their working careers in occupations possessing a more definite Welsh slant. They have returned in order, one might say, to work for Wales.

This may be in jobs involving a responsibility for Welsh sections of a broader-based UK industry, or in occupations which contribute to the way of life in their communities, or, more crucially, in positions which have as their objectives the strengthening of Welsh culture, language and education.

Both individuals featured in this chapter were curious to sample life 'abroad' in England, or even further afield, but being very much Welsh at heart they were more than happy to return, and in one case carefully ensured that any employment outside of Wales was for a limited time period only. Work commitments weren't going to keep her away from Wales and family for long. Wales was most definitely home.

Cledwyn Davies

Whilst working in advertising, one of my clients was the Post Office, with the main client contact being Cledwyn Davies, a native of Llansteffan in Carmarthenshire.

Cledwyn soon afterwards returned to Wales, gaining promotion to become the marketing manager for Wales and the Marches Postal Board, based in Cardiff. He was happy with the social side and the 'buzz' of London, but as a Welshman he could not forsake the opportunity to work in Wales, with the added kudos of being marketing manager for the whole of Wales and the Marches.

Subsequently Cledwyn looked for his own business to run, and he and his wife acquired the village post office in Llangain, Carmarthenshire, near to his Llansteffan birth place. And finally, on selling the business, he became marketing and innovation manager for Coleg Sir Gâr in Llanelli, helping develop the marketing skills of the next generation.

Cledwyn's early childhood mirrors that of previously-mentioned West Walian, Huw Jones.

Cledwyn's father, following an accident on a farm in Pont-Henri in the Gwendraeth Valley, convalesced with his sister in Llansteffan and 'never went back home'. It was here that he met Cledwyn's mum, who was in service on a nearby farm. He subsequently became a foreman at a milk factory in Carmarthen.

Llansteffan was very much a community where 'everybody knew everybody'. It still is, but people now have to make it happen. In the past, such closeness occurred more organically with less movement of population, and social life centred on the village and its chapels, churches, school and pubs.

Llansteffan, being a seaside holiday village, was quite English-speaking. His mother's village of Llanybri, a little further inland, was on the other hand, definitely a Welsh-speaking village. But the main local town of Carmarthen had an English bias. As pointed out so vividly in Byron Rogers's book *Three Journeys*, Carmarthen was a garrison town populated from outside by the English many centuries back.

Cledwyn, like Huw, spoke Welsh at home until he was five, but then went to English-speaking schools in Llansteffan and Carmarthen. He has subsequently retained less of his Welsh than Huw Jones in Pontarddulais.

Cledwyn, following in my footsteps, read international politics and economics at Aberystwyth University, and like me, was quite happy to seek employment amidst the bright lights of London.

At that time he saw the Welsh as parochial, focused on their own geographical environment, without any aspirations to move. He observes that the first black person he ever met was in university at Aberystwyth.

Working in London, he was quite happy to exploit his Welshness as a point of difference to gain more recognition. Cledwyn's name, strange sounding to English ears, was part of this differentiation. The only other person called Cledwyn of whom colleagues were aware was politician Cledwyn Hughes, and often when introduced to business associates, Cledwyn would accidentally acquire the surname 'Hughes'.

Cledwyn's first place of residence was Earls Court, followed by Barnes, Brentford and then South Croydon. He hated the last named, finding it an anonymous commuter belt with masses of houses and little in the way of green spaces. Neighbours were strangers.

As a result he moved to Chiswick, and immediately prior to returning to Wales lived in Twickenham, which offered far more in the way of plentiful open spaces (Richmond Park, Barnes Common) and of course the close proximity of the London Welsh rugby club.

He had also by now met Suzanne, his wife-to-be, who came to Wales with him on his promotion to marketing manager for Wales and the Marches.

After three years, however, Cledwyn became disenchanted with his responsibilities in Cardiff, his brief becoming more sales force than marketing oriented. He could have returned to London but with their first child, Rhys, six months old, Cledwyn and Suzanne no longer wanted the big city life. So Cledwyn looked for a business to run, searching mainly in the area west of Neath, being, as he puts it, 'a West Wales boy' at heart.

As luck would have it, the village post office in Llangain, just outside Llansteffan, became available. It was a 'win-win' situation, representing the best business opportunity they had explored, with Cledwyn's roots also in the area. He felt comfortable knowing the people and the area, and being a local boy could only have a positive influence on trade. Suzanne also liked the area. She had become familiar with it when visiting

Cledwyn's mother, they had many friends in the area, and they were actually married in Llansteffan Church.

After eleven years, Cledwyn and Suzanne finally sold the business in 1998 and have since found a lovely spot to live, in Nantgaredig, in the Tywi valley just east of Carmarthen.

Cledwyn's reminiscences of his various homes in Wales indicate how the physical geography of an area or village can have a profound effect on the local way of life.

Whilst working in Cardiff, Cledwyn and Suzanne lived in Llantwit Vardre, still then a mining village, between Llantrisant and Pontypridd. With houses on top of each other, this was a close valley community with very much its own camaraderie, even its own dialect.

Llangain was also a very friendly community. When an ex-London flatmate, a Scot originally from Glasgow, visited the family, he was astonished to find every passing motorist tooting his horn, and people continually stopping to talk in the street. For him, this was a culture completely alien to London and Glasgow.

During their time in Llangain the village expanded, with two new housing developments. These were occupied by a mix of young families and retired people, often of English descent. But it was difficult for these newcomers to ignore the Welsh language and culture, with many 'English' children becoming Welsh speakers after attending the village school.

The family finally moved to Nantgaredig, falling in love with a property in a lovely spot in the Tywi valley. But the village, typical of many in the Tywi and Gwendraeth valleys, is what geographers love to call a ribbon development, stretching for miles without a true centre. So there was little conversation on the streets, especially after the Post Office closed. But there were still the hoots of passing cars, and a family involvement in the community, at least when the children were still at school.

The church was another element which contributed to the community, with two within the parish, albeit both two miles outside the village. One provided English-language services, whilst the other was bilingual. Cledwyn's family attended the bilingual church, where services were led by a vicar who had taught himself Welsh specifically to offer bilingual worship. The congregation could themselves choose to say the Lord's Prayer in the language with which they were most comfortable.

Despite the lack of a geographical heart, the Nantgaredig community has also more recently grown stronger following the revitalising of the local pub by a new owner, and the success of Nantygaredig RFC in gaining two consecutive promotions to National League Three West B.

So how much has Cledwyn's family involved itself in Welsh language and culture on his return to Wales?

With an English mum, the children were unlikely to speak Welsh at home. Firstborn Rhys was taught Welsh in school, can speak it to a degree, but his default language is English. Second child Rhodri initially experienced some learning difficulties, so it was decided that it would be simpler if he were to concentrate on just the one language, namely English. It proved to be the right decision, with Rhodri eventually going on to university.

Youngest child Catrin, however, attended Welsh-medium primary and secondary schools in Nantgaredig, and has mainly Welsh-speaking friends. She loves the Welsh language, but rather than follow many of her friends to Cardiff University, she decided instead to experience the world outside Wales, choosing to study medicine in Sheffield.

An added dimension is of course the increase of immigration to the area in recent years, but Cledwyn is happy to accommodate this. He is aware of different accents and languages as he pushes his trolley around Tesco, now with its Polish food counter. But for him this is not a problem. The majority of immigrants appear to be adjusting to the local way of life, and through the schools many of their children are learning Welsh and absorbing Welsh culture and heritage. Several of the staff at the local Ivy Bush Hotel, where Cledwyn's Rotary Club meets, are foreign. They are also extremely professional, friendly and good at their jobs. And during the 2016 European Football Championship, a Portuguese worker actually confessed to Cledwyn his dilemma re whom to support in the semi-final – Wales or their opponents, his country of origin.

Despite living for a time in London, having family in Birmingham and loads of local friends from England, Cledwyn finds it difficult to identify a generic English character, as there are so many different English regions, with the Cockneys, Geordies, Brummies and Scousers, like the Welsh, all having their individual cultural identity.

And whilst he knows it's a sweeping generalisation, as a complete nation he detects a certain arrogance in their attitude towards the world, which leaves the Welsh feeling a bit 'hard done by'. He tells the story of a fellow member complaining in the locker room of the Carmarthen Golf Club about English rugby coach Graham Rowntree querying referee Steve Walsh's penalising of the English scrum in the 30–6 Welsh demolition of England at the Millennium Stadium in 2013.

'Don't talk to me about that. Bloody English. So bloody arrogant. We've sent men to shed their blood for them. It's enough to put me off my game!'

But like many of the returning exiles to whom I have spoken, Cledwyn does not support total independence and is more in favour of a federal state. He believes Wales couldn't sustain itself, for example, in terms of defence or social welfare, but is in favour of a National Assembly. It gives the Welsh people an identity and focus in terms of controlling their own destiny, and believes that Wales has benefited from the greater European funding that has been generated as a result, and we are no worse off than we have been under the complications of the Barnett Formula.

But also, like many others, Cledwyn recognises that Wales hasn't made the most of the Assembly. His politics are 'pink', and he believes that the PR voting system makes it difficult to have a majority party in power who can push through their agenda. He doubts the capabilities of some of the AMs and senior officials, and feels there has been a mushrooming in the number of civil servants. But he wouldn't want Wales to be without an Assembly.

In terms of Wales's representation in the media, Cledwyn, like Huw Jones, doesn't support my own more negative views. As a 'region' with 5% of the British population, he believes we receive our fair share of programming in national media, and cites examples on *Channel 4 News* (including the coverage of Swansea City's Capital One Cup victory at Wembley in 2011) and the once-a-week or fortnightly inclusion of Welsh Assembly events in Radio 4's *Today in Parliament*. He also points out that the *Western Mail* can be accessed online (now it isn't circulated in England) and the *Sunday Times* has a Welsh edition (although as far as I can see this only amounts to an alternative sports headline, plus two extra pages of Welsh rugby coverage, and a leader article or two by various Welsh politicians. It doesn't even extend to providing regional TV schedules).

I also have to say in my defence that if the overall conclusion of media fairness is correct, it is only as a result of fifty years of minority group campaigning, including a threatened Gwynfor Evans hunger strike.

Cledwyn's own social life centres on what I perceived as the quintessentially British, if not English, Carmarthen Golf Club and Carmarthen Tywi Rotary Club. As mentioned earlier, I have now been informed that the Rotary is in fact a North-American creation which sees itself as an international service organisation designed to bring together business and professional leaders to provide humanitarian services, encourage ethical standards and help build goodwill and peace in the world.

Anticipating the stereotypical Rotary image of stuffy old men doing lunch, Cledwyn has been pleasantly surprised by the broad cross-section of society they represent, finding them a good mix and a 'good laugh'. And Cledwyn has become highly active, including standing as president, treasurer and running an annual charity boxing dinner which raises thousands for charity, and for which he has become quite well known locally.

Cledwyn is also forever volunteering to assist local causes and institutions, including being treasurer of the Carmarthen branch of Guide Dogs for the Blind. In addition, because of his love of history, and Welsh history in particular, he is a Carmarthen town guide during the summer months, and also a volunteer with the National Trust, leading 'Hidden House Tours' at Newton House in the wonderful Dinefwr Park near Llandeilo. He was even selected as a volunteer driver for the 2015 Rugby World Cup matches held in Cardiff. Where does he find the time to actively support all these worthwhile local causes?

As far as involvement in Welsh culture is concerned, Cledwyn has left this to his daughter Catrin, who played in the school orchestra at the Urdd Eisteddfod, and his English-born wife, Suzanne.

Suzanne has always been community-driven, running a cub group when they lived in Llantwit Vardre, and helping set up the church Sunday School in Llangain.

Suzanne is also musical. The only one of eight siblings to show any interest in music, she played the violin whilst at school in Birmingham. Then later, when packed off by her parents to the Salvation Army to give them a bit of peace and quiet on a Sunday afternoon, she learnt to play the euphonium.

With more free time now the children have left school, Suzanne has become very much involved in Wales's musical tradition. She sang with the Myrddin Chorale before her voice began to struggle, plays in the Ystradgynlais Brass Band, and the Carmarthen Symphonic Wind Band, of which Cledwyn is now the president.

She is now naturalised Welsh. Not a natural linguist, she has made two or three attempts to learn the language without great success, although she understands enough to know roughly what is being said around her, especially if it is about her! She sings in Welsh quite comfortably, and even shouts for Wales on the rugby field. She has sung and played at numerous

National Eisteddfodau, and watches music programmes avidly on S4C, including the regular *Noson Lawen*.

In an article in *The Times* about cricketer Fawad Ahmed, who has played for Australia subsequent to leaving Pakistan, where he was reportedly threatened by the Taliban, Matthew Syed writes: 'It is worth stating that immigrants often have a greater pride in their adopted nation than those who grew up here. In that sense, the emotional dimension of nationalism is not about anything as simplistic as place of birth – John McEnroe was born in Germany and Sir Bradley Wiggins in Belgium. Rather, it is about taking seriously the idea that nationalism can... only work when sufficient numbers care about their country.'

Cledwyn himself spent the last years of his working life as marketing and innovation manager for Coleg Sir Gâr, the local further and higher education college, working with local industries to develop skills through training, and, with the help of Welsh Assembly funding, developing a culture of entrepreneurship and innovation at the college and beyond.

Apparently there is no Welsh word for 'entrepreneur'. Not that there is in English. But there is very much a need for the development of such skills to generate new industry in Wales in the aftermath of the decline of its heavy industry.

The Welsh have a funny attitude towards success in business. Cledwyn speaks of a Llansteffan boy setting up his own IT company before selling it for £100 million. On his return to the village some locals could only exhibit signs of jealousy towards him. 'Did you see him last weekend showing off in his white Rolls Royce?' they would mutter amongst themselves.

Broadcaster Huw Edwards, once asked by the *Daily Mail* to reminisce about his schooldays in Llanelli, claimed to retain only warm memories, apart from a failure he felt to encourage ambition.

But Coleg Sir Gâr seems to be making progress on all fronts. With 12,000 students spread across five county campuses, and 850 teaching and support staff, it offers academic qualifications,

help to those with learning difficulties, plus apprenticeships and business partnerships with local industry. It has achieved a string of learning, training and sporting awards.

Cledwyn's role as marketing and innovation manager at the college required him to be conversant, to a degree, in Welsh, and he has been in a perfect position to witness the issues involved in the promotion of Welsh as a living language.

In the 1960s Cledwyn's attitude was similar to mine, viewing the painting out of English road signs by *Cymdeithas yr Iaith Gymraeg* (the Welsh Language Society) as the work of extremists. What was the point of having everything translated into Welsh?

Like myself, Cledwyn's views have undergone a sea change. We both now appreciate what this small group of protesters have achieved across fifty years to preserve the language, and by default, the culture that is Wales. Our identity shouldn't be lost, even if it means all official forms, including those provided by the Post Office whilst he worked there, being bilingual.

But Cledwyn also appreciates that this creates problems for non-Welsh speakers, amongst whom he includes himself. He detests the academic, intellectual snobbery that partly surrounds the understanding of the language.

Whilst at Coleg Sir Gâr he, along with other staff, was asked to complete a SWOT analysis (Strengths, Weaknesses, Opportunities, Threats) on the preservation of the Welsh language. The organiser of the analysis patronisingly assumed that there 'couldn't possibly be any weaknesses'. Cledwyn immediately corrected her, pointing out how those who were less fluent in Welsh were frequently looked down on if they lapsed into English when attempting to speak in Welsh.

Cledwyn, however, also speaks positively of representing the college at meetings regarding sponsorship of the Urdd National Eisteddfod, which were always held in Welsh, and of the chairman being quite understanding and positive about Cledwyn's struggles to communicate in Welsh, not criticising his occasional use of English words. There is still hope for

a Welsh society which has the space to accommodate and integrate both Welsh and non-Welsh speakers.

Rhian Jones

I met Rhian when she became the very first professional CEO to be appointed by the London Welsh Centre in London's Kings Cross. During her tenure between 2012 and 2014, the centre thrived socially, culturally and in terms of revenue as a meetings venue for corporate organisations and as an excellent rehearsal space for many London theatre productions. The centre also became firmly established as the place in London to watch Six Nations rugby, attracting hundreds of supporters, including a fair sprinkling of Welsh students studying in London. The atmosphere was second only to the stadia themselves.

Rhian hails originally from Talybont in Ceredigion, part of a first language, Welsh-speaking family, going to both a local Welsh-medium primary school and a Welsh-language secondary school in Aberystwyth. She also had an early interest in languages in general, and through the medium of Welsh, she studied French, German and business studies through to A-level before going on to Swansea University, and a year in Strasbourg as an Erasmus student, to read for a joint honours degree in the same three subjects. She admits, however, to Liverpool also being on her shortlist of universities.

Her mother was a secretary at the Welsh primary school, subsequently performing the same role at the Welsh Department in Aberystwyth University. Her father was an animal-health inspector.

Historically the family had always been Ceredigion-based, with Rhian's dad hailing from Tre Taliesin, the next village north along the A487, and her mother coming from Llanrhystud, just south of Aberystwyth.

The Welsh language clearly identifies Rhian as Welsh. It's almost her whole identity, not just a part of it. It's who she is. It's her everyday life. To quote Rhian, 'The Welsh language is everything.'

She hardly spoke any English before she went to university. When speaking to many of her friends it would almost seem alien to use the English language. It would be a different conversation. And she would hate to speak to her nieces in any language other than Welsh. When at home for an evening she will generally watch at least one programme on S4C.

Many of her group, including herself, have jobs which involve the Welsh language. And when she writes reports in Welsh, she admits to sometimes not being able to call to mind what would be the equivalent word in English. Although, sod's law, the reverse can sometimes happen when writing or speaking in English too.

So in the continuing debate between Welsh and non-Welsh speakers, the first conclusion to draw from Rhian's upbringing and way of life is that we cannot possibly take away the birthright of these Welsh speakers to speak their first and natural language, however small a minority they may be.

I have mentioned earlier that Roger Banner of Monmouth and Aberystwyth University had been uncertain about the policy of having a hall of residence exclusively for Welsh-speaking students. Rhian has no such doubts:

'I agree with the principle that Welsh speakers (including learners) should have access to a shared space that enables them to speak Welsh without fear of, a) being accused of alienating non-Welsh speakers and, b) being alienated for speaking Welsh. It's about the right for students to go about their daily lives through their language of choice, and for many the language they are most comfortable with.'

Secondly, if we believe that encouraging the learning of Welsh is a necessary part of preserving our heritage, and we plan to take seriously the attempt to create a bilingual society, Rhian's CV is a clear indication that learning the language can also be of great benefit in the pursuance of a career.

Rhian didn't set out to follow a career which involved the Welsh language, but her ability to speak it has certainly been a major factor in her being selected for several positions.

After a gap year travelling and working around Australia, New Zealand and Malaysia, her first 'proper job' was as a research assistant for an Aberystwyth PR company which partly promoted itself as being one of the few such companies in Wales which offered a bilingual service.

She then went off to France for two years to teach Welsh at the University of Rennes II in Brittany. One of her proudest moments was organising a trip for her Breton students to come to Wales, which not only helped improve their language skills but also taught them something about Welsh culture. Most of them even made it to the summit of Snowdon (and back down), despite the terrible fog.

There followed a short spell at the Swansea University marketing department translating websites into Welsh, before a five-year stint as an education coordinator at Shelter Cymru, also in Swansea. This involved teaching young people about achieving the transition to independent living, giving them a better understanding of the effects of homelessness and their rights if this became their situation. The coordinator worked with a range of partners including schools, local authorities, youth services and the Welsh Government's NEET ('Not in Education, Employment or Training') strategy. The work was targeted, local, and again bilingual.

The next step in Rhian's career was her move to London to become CEO of the London Welsh Centre, where being able to speak Welsh was again a decided, though not essential, advantage in dealing with the large number of Welsh speakers, of all generations and backgrounds, amongst the association's members. The centre in addition has a large Welsh learners' programme enrolling up to 100 learners each year.

The Welsh-language element of much of Rhian's career has provided her with the opportunity to travel to France and London, in addition to her gap year in the southern hemisphere.

She was quite happy to experience the world outside the small-village environment that was Talybont, but in her career planning, although that has been fairly unstructured, she quite

consciously knew that each sojourn 'abroad' would only be for a limited time period. In her head she knew she was bound to return. She is a home-bird at heart.

Generally she looks back at her time in London with fondness. She always knew she was going back to Wales so she couldn't really say that any feeling of *hiraeth* kicked in, and she tried to make the most of her time there and take in as many opportunities as possible. And of those there were many, with the post of CEO at the centre opening doors to many prestigious high profile events and places. Dinner with Carwyn Jones and Huw Edwards! Photo opportunities with the British Lions!

The things she liked about London were also the things she didn't like: the chaos, the sheer scale, the anonymity (outside of Gray's Inn Road).

London hadn't actually been on the to-do list, the job opportunity had just appeared. She was never completely happy being away from her family. Her parents were almost upset to see her going to London and I remember her mother in fact visiting her on a regular basis. And her father, on one of his visits, can even lay claim to having painted the railings outside the London Welsh Centre.

She missed her friends. She often had to miss out on occasions such as a friend's wedding. And being geographically closer to her family had become more important over the years. Her brothers had expanded the Jones empire, and she had become conscious of her parents getting older.

It wouldn't kill her to live in England, especially if she were to meet an English millionaire, but the older she gets the harder it has become. And she's only in her late thirties.

So the next and most recent job opportunity has brought Rhian back to Swansea. In fact she had retained the house she owns in Wales whilst working in London: a terraced house in the working-class district of St Thomas in East Swansea.

She currently commutes to Carmarthen to Y Coleg Cymraeg Cenedlaethol where she is a development officer for the arts and humanities.

The Coleg is about supporting and promoting Welsh-medium higher education, which includes funding research and lecturers, developing resources and encouraging students to study subjects through the medium of Welsh. The job involves the academic planning of modules, and even degrees, through bringing people together from the various universities; organising the practical stuff, such as booking venues and transport for meetings and residential courses; and campaigning in schools to make sure students get the message early.

The work involves much travel around Wales which also gives her the opportunity to call in on her parents and her brothers, who both live within a few miles of the family home. They joke that perhaps this time she'll stay for more than just half an hour.

Rhian grew up taking the Welsh language for granted. 'It's just who I am.' And she never sits down with friends to talk seriously about the language. But she is thinking about it more now, because of the job she is doing persuading young people of the benefits of Welsh.

She thinks that with the growth of legislation, having a bilingual workforce is key, and it is also only fair that Welsh speakers have the opportunity to work in their chosen language.

Her commitment to both the language and the care of the Welsh people also now extends to a considerable number of extracurricular activities.

Her current voluntary positions include being a director of Menter Iaith Abertawe (Tŷ Tawe), the Swansea branch of an organisation which promotes the Welsh language through teaching, translation services and social activities. She loves the sense of community generated, knowing personally all the people who gather socially every Friday night. There is something nice about everybody knowing everybody, with typically fewer degrees of separation between individuals in Wales than found elsewhere.

She is also a governor of Ysgol Gynradd y Cwm, the Welsh-

language school in Bonymaen, and a trustee of the Swansea Young Single Homeless Project (SYSHP).

She believes those who campaign for the Welsh language do really good work, but carrying placards is not for her. She is a quiet campaigner doing what she can for the language and the community. She took the language for granted while growing up but now thinks about it a lot more because of the job she is doing. She wants to contribute.

In other ways she is not typically Welsh. She isn't particularly musical and she grew up going to the village church rather than chapel. But she does have a love of sport.

She played hockey, netball and badminton at school and county level. She captained the Welsh Universities women's football team at the BUSA Games in Belfast in 1998 (actually there when the Good Friday Agreement was signed). Since graduating, her pursuits have been more individual, including, to date, eight marathons, around fifteen half-marathons, several 10ks, a few sprint triathlons and charity bike rides, most notably the 2011 Cardiff–Paris ride to raise money for Shelter Cymru. How does she find the time?

Her eldest brother was obsessed with Ian Rush, so she grew up a big Liverpool football fan, although recently she has supported Swansea City in their rise to the top echelon, visiting the Liberty Stadium five times in a season. She even watched the Ospreys when she first moved to the east side of Swansea.

She loves being Welsh. She loves the Welsh people. She finds us honest, warm and friendly, although like Alan Litherland in Criccieth, and Peter Lane's view of Wales west of Swansea, she finds people in small-village rural Wales more cautious in their outlook. People talk in the street in Swansea; they tell you their life story. At the same time there is more anonymity. In Mid Wales everyone knows everybody and people are more guarded about their business. But there is still a warmth there.

So as a compromise she has settled in Swansea, which she now calls home. Her family thus jokingly request her to refer to Talybont as 'home home', or more precisely *'adre, adre'*.

She doesn't hate the English, only finding some of them arrogant; at least John Inverdale. And taking part in a fantasy rugby competition at work she struggled emotionally with the thought of incorporating any English players in her team, despite their recent successes. But in the end, she says, 'being a 'Cardi', winning the money became more important!'

Yet it was an irrelevance to ask her whether she regarded herself as Welsh or British, and whether or not Wales should have a devolved government.

But she is still aware of deficiencies in the Welsh character. She sees us as unambitious, more afraid to take risks than, say, the Irish, and too capable of 'cutting off our nose to spite our face'. Those failing to land contracts or gain selection will 'throw their toys out of the pram' and refuse to lend their support to the winning organisation or person. The Welsh are notorious for bickering in committees.

Yet we are politically apathetic when it comes to Wales itself. Turnouts at Welsh Assembly elections are always low.

She appreciates that all government is difficult. The Assembly has much to learn, but it is too easy to be critical.

Rhian accepts that conflicts often exist in matters Welsh, and very much adopts a pragmatic and common-sense approach to Welsh-language issues.

She recognises that promotion of the language will always be a balancing act. People must never be thought of as more or less Welsh because they can or cannot speak the language. It is good to have people who care about keeping up standards for the language, but at the same time there has to be a middle ground. Young people must never be led to think that their language isn't good enough. And there should always be language tutors there to help.

The number studying the Welsh language itself is decreasing. The subject matter needs more of a modern focus with an emphasis on Welsh skills in the workplace.

Children are reverting to English once out of school. On the other hand there are centres which encourage and champion

the learning of Welsh, with parents even learning the language to keep up with their children. And Rhian feels that the award of Learner of the Year could highlight some of the real characters from this general population rather than the more obvious choices amongst people who have moved to Wales or visitors from Patagonia.

The preservation of the language is in good hands if there are people like Rhian prepared not only to make a significant contribution to its upkeep and expansion, but who also appreciate that the views and requirements of others, including non-Welsh speakers and those of the new younger generation, need to be taken into account.

Working for the Valleys

HOWEVER MUCH I try to define a unique Welsh identity I obviously have to recognise that even a country as small as Wales can never be a single homogeneous unit. The mountains of Mid Wales, plus the creation of east–west-only travel arteries, has meant that for centuries there was little communication between North and South Wales. At the same time, the Valleys of South Wales have always been more concerned with addressing the socialist needs and rights of the coal and steel workers than the promotion of Welsh nationalism.

And then there is the small matter of the views of Welsh speakers versus non-Welsh speakers. Welshness can obviously mean different things to different people.

This chapter focuses on a one-time South Wales Valleys resident, who, despite forsaking what he describes as his 'boring' existence in the Valleys for a more exciting life in the clubs, pubs and music industry of Camden, North London, has still been motivated to create an annual music, arts and literature festival in his home town of Blackwood.

It was a difficult environment in which to grow up. His eleventh birthday coincided with the start of the Miners' Strike, which lasted from March 1984 to March the following year. But he loves the town and the people. 'They are my people, you have got to love them.' And he wants to give something back to them.

Yet he also believes that the promotion of the festival has been better handled externalised from Blackwood and Wales, to provide clarity of vision, 'to think outside the box', to broaden the range of artists and generate interest and funding from outside of Wales. Only as a result of that have those within the more cautious local environment been happy to become involved in the concept.

He has in one sense still returned to Wales, but in a far more exotic and motivating way than just living there. And he has demonstrated that for Wales to succeed as a nation it also needs to look outside its borders both for inspiration and for support.

Iain Richards

From 2012 to 2014 Iain Richards was cultural development officer of the London Welsh Centre in London's Gray's Inn Road, a position funded by the Ashley Family Foundation. He was a colleague of CEO Rhian Jones.

As members we thought of him as Blackwood's tourist officer, so often did he mention the place. Iain ran many successful quiz evenings with his usual style and charisma, the one idiosyncrasy being the frequency with which the town of Blackwood featured in the questions. The first such question involved knowing how far Blackwood was from Tredegar. By the fourth quiz he even had the nerve to ask how many questions had involved Blackwood in the previous quizzes.

Iain was raised in Blackwood, in the Sirhowy valley, offspring of three generations of miners. Both his mam and dad came from the neighbouring Rhymney Valley, their families moving to Blackwood during the housing boom of the 1950s and 60s. They met in the Red Lion pub on Blackwood High Street. Iain's grandparents on one side of the family lived less than a mile away, and the other set lived in the next street in a house now occupied by his brother and family.

The neighbourhood was thus a very close-knit community, with its solidarity nurtured by the Miners' Strike of 1984. This obviously had a significant effect on Iain. He was aware of his father's presence on the picket line, and his attendance at marches as far away as London and Sheffield. Along with the other miners, his dad would also take his turn twice a week outside Tesco collecting money for the strike.

Iain was a more-than-useful footballer, with his father

his number one supporter. But as luck would have it, on the weekend Iain scored his first hat-trick, his father had to be on duty outside Tesco.

Times were strange. Without work, Iain's dad would be around the house most of the time. The local Islwyn council provided the children with their lunches served at the school. So even in the holidays Iain would have to return to school to be fed. His mother, meanwhile, could be found every Thursday afternoon, along with a dozen other miners' wives, at Blackwood Workingmen's Club, preparing food parcels for up to fifty other families.

The net effect of all these experiences was that Iain was radicalised and politicised from an early age. He is unquestionably on the left of politics forever. 'This is non-negotiable.'

The 'enemy' was the Tory government under Thatcher, and this political identity had in fact more in common with the miners of Derbyshire and Yorkshire than with the people of rural or North Wales. And today, having spent most of his adult life in London, he also has more English friends.

There have been times, however, when he has become disillusioned with the watered-down 'socialism' of New Labour, and looked to the equally left-wing Plaid Cymru, but in his eyes Plaid never focused on the key issues, concentrating more on the goal of independence along with the wholesale promotion of the Welsh language.

He wishes he could speak Welsh and that Blackwood was Welsh-speaking. Most of the local place names are in fact very Welsh. And he feels that the Rhymney and Sirhowy Valleys were initially blitzed out of Welshness more than neighbouring valleys by the sheer volume of coalmines and the greater proportion of English management brought in to run them. More than in the Rhondda Valleys, for example.

But now he fears that non-Welsh speakers, the vast majority of the population, are being marginalised. There are many media jobs available in Cardiff for which many of those applying are rejected because they cannot speak Welsh. How

do the hirers know that the 20% who speak Welsh are the best people for the job?

The third string to Iain's radical bow is his feeling that in any case Wales is too Cardiff-centric, especially in relation to the Valleys. The transport links are still 'crap'. Iain feels that the new Welsh Assembly seemed to spend most of its first ten years just building roads up and down the Valleys, but the concept of a new city region is doomed without also the completion of a metro system. To talk about a new metropolis is premature until this system is actually accomplished, yet apparently Cardiff Council have already undertaken a promotional tour to New York.

To his mind, the publicity is overblown, with Welsh flags everywhere. Cardiff, in a European context, is not a big city. Wales is a country of small villages, with not enough work to go around.

Socially, however, he likes what's happening in Cardiff, and its compactness is a positive in this regard.

The WRU he tars with the same brush as Cardiff Council: middle class, middle-aged and elitist. Their recent campaign claiming that rugby defines us, gets on his nerves. Who gives them the right to define our cultural identity? It's not our national sport. On whatever criteria, paying customers, viewing figures, number of players, football is bigger. And the formation of four rugby regions to the exclusion of the Valleys has clearly failed. To assume that the Gwent valleys would support Newport, that Pontypridd would support Cardiff, was a huge error. The move has just served to alienate people.

Like the rest of us, however, he does not know the answer to how Welsh rugby should be structured to successfully meet the financial demands of the new professional era.

So what was Iain like, growing up in his teens?

School didn't interest him. He didn't like being told what to do, and found the whole experience boring. Even going to gigs in Cardiff and Newport proved to be a big effort, given the state of public transport. His main interests were sport (he

played for Gwent Under 19s in football and rugby, and had a trial for Swindon Town), playing the guitar and, surprisingly, literature.

The catalyst for this last preoccupation was in fact the music of the Manic Street Preachers, formed in Blackwood itself in 1986. He not only identified with their furious rock sound but also with the critical social lyrics about 'culture, alienation, boredom and despair', to quote the words of the Manics' *Little Baby Nothing*, also the title of the film documentary about the band by Kieran Evans. They offered him both a leftist politicisation and an intellectual lyrical style. He could quote you every word from every song from every record. They were like 'a breath of fresh air'.

Iain didn't bother with A-levels, preferring to use his free bus pass to visit the record and guitar shops of Newport. In his own words, he was 'no role model for aspiring students'. Leaving school early, he instead enrolled in Cross Keys College on a two-year computer studies course, and 'miraculously' got into the Swansea Institute of Higher Education (now the Swansea Metropolitan University) to study business studies. He also spent two summers in America, on the second occasion undertaking some football coaching.

He became quite depressed for a couple of years, spending his time reading novels and dreaming of being a rock star. Then after a period sorting himself out in Birmingham, in his mid-twenties, he hit the 'galaxy' that was Camden Town. This he describes as 'a glorious time'. 'The boredom of Wales was extinguished in a microsecond.'

For the first few years in Camden he worked in bars, in the organic food industry and at music venues. At this stage, Wales was a lost entity to him. But as he got older he became curious as to how he could reconnect with Wales, and rugby turned out to be the initial catalyst.

By now, through college and work experience, he had acquired organisational skills and an ability to network for contacts. He became a fundraiser for SKRUM (Swaziland

Kids Rugby Mission) and subsequently a fundraiser and events organiser for the Lesotho Rugby Academy.

In 1985, an independent charity, Dolen Cymru Wales Lesotho Link, had been set up to foster a unique country-to-country link between Wales and Lesotho.

The link was created partly because of the similarities between the two countries: similar in population size, both mountainous (Lesotho is known as 'The Mountain Kingdom', 'The Kingdom in the Sky') and both dominated by a larger neighbour (South Africa in Lesotho's case). But Lesotho also has 25% of its population living with HIV/Aids, the third highest in the world, and a life expectancy of only 47.

One objective of the country-to-country link was to educate children and encourage them to reach their potential. With this in mind, a friend of Iain's, Dan Aylward, a British government economist working in Lesotho, set up the Federation of Lesotho Rugby, together with the Lesotho Rugby Academy. The latter set out to use rugby as a means of educating children about HIV, gender equality and human rights.

Iain's major contribution was the creation of the Lesotho Sevens, to be played each year in Blackwood, involving a festival weekend of schools, youth and ladies rugby, together with an eight-team competition for elite Gwent and Glamorgan clubs.

For the SKRUM charity, Iain also organised a question-and-answer session between himself and Welsh international Mike Phillips, just after Mike had returned from being with Wales in New Zealand for the 2011 World Cup. The women supporters of London's rugby clubs were queuing up for tickets to see him.

Iain approached the London Welsh Centre as a possible venue for the event, but with a narrowness of vision, the centre claimed that priority had to be given to their own choirs' rehearsals and events on the suggested dates. However, two weeks later, the then chairman, Alex Meredith, contacted Iain, sending him an application form for the position of cultural development manager at the centre.

Iain's ambitions involved modernising the centre's programme to appeal to London's younger Welsh population, including the showcasing of exciting current music. He and Rhian Jones also succeeded in making the centre the place to watch Six Nations rugby, Iain setting up interviews with several London reporters to publicise the venue. Hundreds packed the centre for each Welsh game and the Brains beer flowed.

In 2013 Iain also had the idea of holding a three-day London Welsh Literature Festival, which incorporated an eclectic mix of literature, music and history including: sessions for children chaired by Martin Dawes, the then Young Peoples Laureate for Wales, along with sessions in Welsh presented by Ifor ap Glyn, subsequently to become the National Poet of Wales.

It also featured the commemoration of the centenary of the Senghenydd mining disaster; readings to celebrate the centenary of the birth of Dylan Thomas; discussions on Welsh identity and Wales, a rugby nation, the latter involving conversations with John Dawes and Owen Sheers, WRU artist in residence, and a presentation by Huw Edwards on modern journalism.

In the field of music there were presentations on the growth of punk, the history of the NME, independent record labels and the Manic Street Preachers; a musical showcase of four of the 12 bands shortlisted for the Welsh Music Prize and an update on the music scene in Cardiff and London.

Iain's showcasing of Welsh music had involved Radio 1 DJ Huw Stephens in regular sessions at the London Welsh Centre. Huw, along with music promoter John Rostron, had also created an annual Welsh Music Prize, to champion the best new music coming out of Wales, and Iain was very honoured to be appointed to the panel of judges for the 2015 prize.

Encouraged by the success of the London festival venture, Iain began to believe that he was also capable of doing something for Blackwood, to produce an event that would make it a creative hub, giving it a much needed sense of civic pride, and also giving its people a tangible sense of excitement, to counter the sensationalist celebrity hype usually associated with today's typical TV entertainment offerings, and the sense of boredom Iain felt existed in his own teenage years.

So was born Velvet Coalmine: a Festival of Writing, Rock'n'Roll and Coal. Iain sought initially to externalise it from Blackwood, to obtain sponsorship and artists from outside of Wales, even outside UK. He formed a limited company for which he achieved funding from such bodies as Comic Relief, The Joe Strummer (from the Clash) Foundation, Performing Rights Society for Music and the Community Foundation in Wales, before attempting to attract local support. Several years in, he now has the complete backing of the council and every school in the district.

It is also interesting to note that he has achieved the support of active business people who have moved from England and settled in Wales. Of the twelve individuals on the sponsorship committee, six are from outside Blackwood, and three are English.

This year's festival (2017) will incorporate a ten-day International Children's Literature Festival and four days focusing on African literature and music.

In 2015 there were fifty bands performing across ten stages. They included the Meat Puppets, an iconic American band and a major influence on superstars Nirvana, who had never before performed in Wales, and Dub War, another well-known rock band for whom Blackwood was their only UK show that year. Also performing were two-piece punk duo, Slaves, who have since emerged as one of Britain's biggest bands.

There was a film festival curated jointly by Nicky Wire of the Manics and BAFTA-winning director Kieran Evans.

Both Senghenydd and the Miners' Strike anniversaries have been commemorated at the festival.

There have been events connected to comedy theatre, music-industry panels and even the Welsh language.

Amongst the various bands performing was Henry's Funeral Shoe, a product of Ystrad Mynach, just down the road from

Blackwood. Iain was, until recently, their manager. His interest was in their sound – the fact that they were local was a bonus.

Iain's management style is European, not even UK, in focus. A Cardiff gig would only be one of sixty on the European tour of a major band. And living in London, he can go to a meeting in Brussels faster than he could get home to Blackwood.

He was disappointed with the pro-Brexit vote in the Valleys. He is only too aware of the level of European investment in Wales that will be lost. He believes the general population have just bought into tabloid propaganda without thinking through the issues that actually affect Wales. And whilst today's population of Blackwood lacks its solidarity of old, with the loss of a common goal and enemy, and the far greater mobility of people, one mustn't forget that the creation of the original solidarity was achieved within a population which also had a high level of immigration. Iain's best friends in school were of Polish and Italian origin. People have more similarities than differences. To quote Iain, 'patriotism is a dangerous game.'

Iain is of the Valleys, and not Welsh nor British, but of Europe. And he is providing the Valleys with something to get involved in, and be proud of, even if this is from a London base.

Cartref

DESPITE BORING THE world with constant claims of Welsh friendliness and, according to my wife, being far happier once I've crossed the Severn Bridge into Wales, I had never seriously envisaged that I would actually end up living back home (*cartref*) in Wales. Both my children are bringing up their families in the Thames Valley, governed by work commitments and the search for a location which guarantees the best education for their offspring. My wife's family are either local to us in Hertfordshire, or even further east in Essex. My wife, in particular, has a host of golf, bridge and painting class friends in Hertfordshire and Essex, and whilst many of my friends are Welsh, they are either wedded to the London Welsh Centre in Kings Cross, or live in West London on the doorstep of London Welsh RFC. There is some truth in the myth that the Welsh, like many nationalities, become more nationalistic in exile than ever they were at home. And as Byron Rogers suggests, there is a substantial 'lunar base of Welshness' in the British capital.

But, suddenly, in the January of 2015, my wife announced that it might be quite nice if we were to move to Wales in a few years' time. She had always liked both the scenery and the humour and friendliness of the people, although for years she had always insisted that the closest to Wales she would countenance living was the Forest of Dean.

My response was that, if we were to move, it was better to do it sooner rather than later. Moving house is stressful at any time, let alone in your seventies.

And now seemed as good a time as any. There were decreasing commitments to tie my wife to the south east of England. Her mother had died a few years earlier, two months short of her 100th birthday. Her daughter, my stepdaughter, had recovered from the threat of cancer, and now had a new boyfriend to share the challenge of bringing up her two children. And we were beginning to fall out of love with the aggressive, selfish world that the village of Radlett, Hertfordshire, had come to represent, with the incessant traffic created by the 4x4-loving local mothers ferrying their children to and from school, and themselves just the few hundred yards to the local shops, plus the greed of local developers building yet another six-bedroom mansion in the garden of an original six-bedroom mansion. Who needs a garden when you can have six bedrooms? So much for David Cameron's 'Big Society' and the creation of affordable housing.

The final selling point was financial. My pension was healthy enough, but any additional savings and shares were rapidly disappearing, and a lot of work was beginning to be needed on the house, according to my project-loving wife. And the one benefit of living in a neighbourhood occupied by the new, get-rich-quick generation is that house prices had rocketed over the last twenty years, placing Radlett in the top ten of desirable UK locations. So we have in fact bought a larger house in Wales for not much more than half the price of our previous Radlett abode.

The house-moving process consisted of two distinct phases. The receiving and placing of offers was almost instantaneous. We received an acceptable offer on our previous house within a weekend of going on the market, and one-and-a-half days of viewing eight houses in our chosen Welsh location produced a home with which we are totally in love.

The signing and exchanging of contracts was, however, the stuff of nightmares and heart attacks. The divorcée seller in Wales wanted out as quickly as possible, and on one occasion threatened to put the house back on the market if agreements were not signed by the following midday. This would have been decidedly ill-advised of her, as all seven other houses we viewed during our search were still unsold six months later.

Signatures weren't in the event immediately forthcoming,

as our purchasers, and their purchasers, were both of the opposite persuasion to our seller, and were of a mind to drag out the proceedings for as long as possible. The purchaser's purchaser disappeared for a week's holiday without leaving any signed documents with his solicitors, and our purchaser chose the eleventh hour to start stipulating requirements and repairs deemed necessary before she was prepared to sign anything.

We placated the vendor with a sob letter of how much we wanted the house and how any delays were not of our doing, and pressured our purchasers into signing by offering £1,000 to cover any repairs or searches they deemed to be necessary.

Exchanges duly took place, but not before the date of completion was moved backwards and forwards on three occasions, making the booking of a removal company a logistical nightmare.

The move itself also did not pass without incident. The first of the removal vans left only three-quarters full to ensure that such a large, and therefore slower, vehicle completed the journey on time, leaving a second smaller van insufficient to accommodate the remainder of our belongings. At the last moment the removal men thus began forcing all manner of household and garden items into both of our cars, and ultimately almost drove off with my wife's car keys still in their possession.

We survived.

The estate agents and solicitors at the two locations were in sharp contrast to each other. The Radlett solicitors, whilst ever so efficient on the surface, were cold and almost disinterested in reaching a conclusion to the deal. If a solicitor down the line wanted information or help, their response was limited to 'no' or 'don't know'. On no account would they show any signs of weakness or a propensity to reach an agreement.

The Radlett estate agents were trendy young businessmen and women who thought everything was 'perfect' or 'super'. The Welsh agents were obviously cheaper, also older and far more approachable, who responded to every new detail with 'there we are then'. I'm only now realising that in fact every South Walian ends every conversation with 'well, there we are then', including my long-standing friend Graham, and even Welsh TV personality Huw Edwards on *BBC News at Ten*.

I had also approached the house-moving process in the long-held belief that estate agents were always the villains of the piece, only coming behind journalists and insurance companies as creatures of public disdain. In the event, the agents worked long hours to ensure deals were reached (their financial rewards motivating this response to a degree), whilst the solicitors never showed any signs of ever being prepared to likewise expedite proceedings, proving themselves to be the single key hindrance to achieving any result. They would email you at 8.30 in the morning with some new vital information and then be uncontactable for the rest of the day. They would take a day's holiday without a word of warning, and without finalising necessary details before they departed. They have become new residents of my personal version of Room 101.

Before arranging two days of house viewings in Wales, we undertook a search of various areas along the South Wales coast in order to arrive at our preferred location. We both like Pembrokeshire, but the county is too distant from family and relatives in England. Llanelli is like too many towns in the Thames Valley: lovely surrounding countryside but a desolate and deprived town centre. We spent several days in West Swansea and the Gower, but found every nice residential area either smothered in traffic or high on a hill, no easy walk to the shops.

We finally settled on the Vale of Glamorgan. Three years earlier I had seen a little of Llantwit Major, the site of that year's National Eisteddfod, and had also stayed at The Bear Hotel in Cowbridge on numerous occasions when attending the Millennium Stadium. Llantwit turned out to be much cheaper than Cowbridge, whilst also offering a direct rail link to Cardiff and Bridgend, stations on the main line to London Paddington, plus a beach on Wales's Heritage Coast.

Cowbridge is an elegant haven of clothes and antique shops, olde worlde pubs and fine eateries – and traffic. The women even dress up just to pop down to the local supermarket. It does happen to be a Waitrose, which was welcomed with open arms by a population that had previously rejected ferociously the advances of Tesco.

Llantwit in contrast has a hippy feel to it, with a boho dress shop, a tattoo parlour and independently-owned rather than large chain supermarkets and restaurants. It also has lots of character, narrow winding streets almost reminiscent of a Cotswold village, and loads of history, being the site of the country's earliest university of learning in the fifth century. St Illtyd's still incorporates elements of an eleventh-century church and the Old Swan Inn dates back to the sixteenth century.

Amazingly, for a population of just 13,000, it has five flourishing town-centre pubs, with sixteen others within a few square miles. It is a real-ale paradise with every pub holding its own beer festival, often involving local microbreweries.

And then there is the rugby club. Situated as it is in the very centre of the town, it functions almost as a community centre, with regular pub hours, holding many special events such as an August Bank Holiday 10k run followed by a 'Party on the Pitch', the town's main 5 November firework display and the start of Santa's Christmas Procession. It's become my second, some might even say, first home.

Neither does Llantwit do that badly for restaurants. There is a wonderful family-run Italian pasta and pizzeria, a wine bar which resembles the hall of a Tudor mansion, run by the ex-chef of the five-star hotel on Cardiff Bay, and the Old Swan Inn which offers a fairly modern cuisine along with takeaway fish and chips. And one can always go the five miles down the road to Cowbridge for more posh nosh if so inclined.

Prices are also lower than in the south east of England. I can buy a pint without breaking into yet another note, and I am forever handing over too many pound coins, imagining the cost to be higher. The household oddjob men almost seem embarrassed to accept a tip. Parking is free in the town centre and at the railway station (although much to the annoyance of the populace, rates in Cardiff and Barry have recently been doubled).

Llantwit seems ideal: it avoids the harshness of many industrial towns, yet also does not exude the sense of one-upmanship and snobbery to be found in those places *The Times* housing supplement persists in proclaiming as the most desirable residences in the UK: usually in the south east of England, although Cowbridge would probably be high on any such Welsh list. Having said that, the Royal Mail has actually identified Llantwit, along with a village in Anglesey, as the most desirable postcodes in which to settle in Wales, although I am not sure on what criteria, even if everyone who has lived here for a period of time is adamant that it is a nice place to live.

We have been overwhelmed by the one quality I have continuously claimed on behalf of the Welsh: friendliness. Every person, every stranger, you pass on the street says hello, often with a smile. When raucous youngsters are blocking the pathway, they politely stand aside and apologise. Members of the rugby club, the golf club, the bridge club, have made us astonishingly welcome. And shop assistants call you 'sweetheart' and 'darling'. Whilst other shoppers in the queue always have a joke or even a life story to tell you.

The place is full of characters. There is a plumber called Dai Gas. A local tiling company goes by the name of Bonny Tiler. One electrician, whilst English, is learning Welsh to keep up with his kids. We conversed in Welsh as he fitted a new kitchen light. And then later I bumped into him in the pub as he delivered a barrel of ale from the microbrewery he runs as a sideline.

As suspected, there is plenty of humour, quite often of the black variety. A fellow rugby-club drinker, encountered in the doctor's waiting room, enquired after my health: 'Dying, are you?'

Yet everyone is always on hand to help everyone. We employed a local lad for an evening to take apart our kitchen in readiness for a major refit. The rugby club grapevine rapidly informed a fellow drinker of our plans, and he immediately offered to take the old units off our hands to use in his garage, and, in return, to transport all the old kitchen appliances to the local tip. On the night two friends showed up to assist him. We didn't need a skip. Just a house full of locals.

My stepson and two of his kitchen-fitter colleagues from Hertfordshire came down for three days to finish the task. Three days of hard work and hard play. They spent two very late evenings making friends in a local karaoke and pool pub, twice receiving lifts back to our house from fellow drinkers and even the pub landlord.

Whilst the acquirer of our old kitchen now loves to show off photographs of these units in his rebuilt garage to all and sundry via his mobile phone.

The train to Cardiff is always full of people talking and laughing. (Although catching the commuter special one evening, one felt the train's atmosphere had reverted to the quietness and solemnity of a London tube carriage. Perhaps rush hours are the same the world over?)

Whilst driving and parking in both Cardiff and Cowbridge can be a nightmare, the roads in and around Llantwit are so quiet. One seldom meets another car at a T-junction. Unfortunately, Llantwit is also the speed-bump capital of the world, with a myriad of them occupying almost every road in the town centre.

The retail parks of Bridgend and Cardiff are again more of a drive away than the shops of Watford or St Albans, but the drive is easy and far more scenically pleasant. Life is no longer a permanent hurry.

It also feels a safe place to live. Kids spend all their time playing in the park that is the rugby club. In contrast teenagers heading for the playing fields of Radlett were always imagined to be up to no good, or taking drugs. Having said that, a fellow Welsh learner at the London Welsh Centre, whose sons attended Atlantic College at St Donats, down the coast from Llantwit, told me there was a perception there that Llantwit had some drug issues. And a barman at the local hotel, on my first visit, expressed his concerns about an area of the town known locally as 'the concrete jungle'.

Most locals tell me that Llantwit's problems are no worse than other towns'. And another local man, whose cousin is a probation officer in Llanelli, argued that Llantwit paled into insignificance in comparison to the wild west of Wales.

From my own perspective, through rose-coloured spectacles, the walk through the playing fields in the evening, watching the boys training under the rugby posts, brings back nostalgic childhood memories. In Radlett, I wouldn't even risk walking through the recreation ground on an evening.

None of the houses we viewed in our house search had burglar alarms. The local jeweller who repaired my wristwatch worked on the watch with his back towards the open shop door. In contrast, to enter my Radlett jewellers required the pressing of the doorbell to request the door to be unlocked. The shop's window had unfortunately been rammed as many as three times in the previous five years.

Every house in my street had a burglar alarm, and most had at some time been burgled. Having said that, my friend who had a second home in Llanelli decided to leave the area because of the level of petty crime. Even the flowers in his garden weren't safe. Maybe there are two sides to every coin?

New best friend Bill, ex-Wasps rugby union player, who permanently inhabits the seat at the end of the rugby club bar, recounts how he seldom locks the back door of his cottage, and as a result discovered one morning, asleep on his sofa, a hungover army captain who had mistaken Bill's cottage for the house of a friend. On Bill's behalf he had earlier taken receipt of a parcel at the front door, which, unknown to him, actually contained £1,000 worth of notes collected for a charity. On being shown the door by Bill, the soldier was unable to lay his hands on the overcoat he claimed to have been wearing on his arrival. Bill duly offered him an old gardening jacket, whilst also pointing him in the right direction to return home to St Athan, the soldier having no idea as to his whereabouts.

The following day the soldier appeared at Bill's cottage to return Bill's coat, duly cleaned, along with a box of chocolates as a thank you gift. His last parting remark was to inform Bill that after a chat with his wife, he realised he had become disenchanted with army life, and enquired of Bill whether he thought that the police force might not offer him a more suitable alternative employment. Bearing in mind the previous night's break-in, Bill thought it appropriate not to comment.

My own neurotic nature continues to actively search for other latent threats to my idyllic small-town existence. Will the brook at the bottom of the garden flood, as it has further upstream in nearby villages? Will the developers obtain planning permission to build 300 houses on the field beyond our garden, currently a pasture for a dozen horses and a particularly scenic backdrop to our house? Will the old RAF camp at St Athan become active again and create a permanent flight path over our home?

Currently neither the old RAF base, nor nearby Cardiff International Airport, send planes over our house. The St Athan base is now used more by the army as opposed to the air force, with the site also serving as a base for air-sea rescue helicopters. And it has just been announced that the main hangar has now been acquired by Aston Martin to build its proposed new car model.

Apparently, in previous times, the presence of RAF servicemen in the area did lend a touch of colour and aggression to the local pub scene on a Saturday night.

But the civilian population itself can be just as wild. Travelling through Cardiff by train one often encounters massive hen parties boarding the train en route to or from an event. They usually take over a whole coach as they loudly continue their drinking. I don't ever remember the last Thameslink train out of St Pancras of an evening ever being quite like this. And it's still only nine o'clock in Cardiff. The Welsh certainly know how to party.

Many ex-RAF personnel have a great affection for Llantwit, and have either settled in, or returned to, the area, in retirement. This is also true of many engineers working out of the large Aberthaw power station.

As a result, the camaraderie in pubs and clubs not only reflects the area's Welshness, but a very cosmopolitan mix of Welsh, English, Scottish and Irish, with the odd South African thrown in for good measure.

Others have said that Wales is not only about its people but its place. And in the Llantwit environment a community of spirit has been achieved which has so far accommodated all newcomers into its folds, albeit mainly Caucasian. In the same way, the population of the South Wales Valleys has seen a huge influx of immigrants, mainly English, Irish and the odd Italian, over the last 100 years. And yet these same Valleys now have the largest percentage of population in Wales who claim to be Welsh. Hopefully the population will continue to recreate itself with the same loyalty and generosity of spirit.

What these more recent immigrants lack, however, is a love of the Welsh language. And this is also true of longstanding locals. The rugby club is not blessed with many Welsh speakers, and many members certainly resent having the language forced down their throats by the authorities.

Many object to the excessive cost involved in ensuring that all public documents are provided in both Welsh and English. And most non-Welsh speakers can recount tales of the intransigence of Welsh speakers in their refusal to speak English. A retired, English-born heart surgeon recounts having to insist that nursing staff in Bronglais Hospital, Aberystwyth, addressed him in English when discussing medical cases on the ward, and one of the rugby club's non-Welsh speaking barmen speaks of a similar stand-off when directing traffic onto the National Eisteddfod site at Llantwit Major, the barman resolutely refusing to open the car park gate until the driver of the car seeking entry was prepared to speak to him in English.

We do have to tread very carefully in our attempts to resurrect our Welsh language.

According to a London Welsh acquaintance, another downside of the perceived friendliness of the Welsh is an excess of gossip and nosiness. We have, however, actually found our cul-de-sac to be a haven of quietness. Neighbours have been helpful and welcoming, but not excessively intrusive. Although compare this to Hertfordshire when, in the week before I left to come to Wales, I met someone in a local pub who claimed to have lived opposite me for the whole of my twenty-one year stay. And I still didn't recognise him.

In Llantwit one does sense that beneath the surface everybody does actually know everything about you. When asked where I lived by someone in the rugby club, I presumed I had to describe the precise location of our street. Then on one occasion I realised that all three companions involved in the conversation not only knew the street but had actually worked on my house in its various stages of development. They could even tell me how my bedroom had been altered over the years. I felt as if I was part of an old *Punch* cartoon, possibly entitled 'the new arrival', in which, unknown to me, the whole bar is pointing at me from behind my back.

Even well-known personalities can't hide. Rugby icon JPR Williams sings in my choir. Ex-Welsh rugby international Simon Hill is my dentist. I've played golf with ex-Cardiff City professional footballer Stephen Grapes. As always, the Welsh social chain is shorter.

And contacts will always be made more rapidly, because, whatever organisation you involve yourself in, people will immediately come over and introduce themselves. Everyone is so welcoming.

And we have got involved.

We attend far more local events than we ever entertained previously in Radlett: the Party on the Pitch on August Bank Holiday; the town's 5 November firework display; the rugby club Christmas lunch (which incorporated both Michael Jackson and Neil Diamond tribute bands!)

We (or at least Gill) undertake far more walks, given the availability of the attractive beaches and cliffs of the Welsh Heritage Coast.

And we visit the theatre and cinema, in Cardiff and Bridgend, just as frequently as we did from our Hertfordshire abode. A 10.40 p.m. last train out of Cardiff is not helpful, but Cardiff Bay and the Bridgend Odeon are easily accessible by car.

We have joined the U3A (University of the Third Age). Gill has joined the St Athan Golf Club, winning a trophy in her very first outing, although not much since, and she is also playing more competitive duplicate bridge at the Llantwit and Pontyclun bridge clubs. She has in addition tried an aqua aerobics class, and started art classes at St Donats College and Cowbridge Community Centre. She has already met several new best friends.

I have naturally joined the rugby club (for the social side, not to play rugby) and the golf club. I've even attempted to learn bridge. And I am playing table tennis weekly with a small group of pensioners, many of whom once played seriously in the Cardiff league. I hold my own, but I have been given a meaningful target to which to aspire by an ex-top league table tennis player who informed me, after proving more than a match for me, that he wasn't bad for the ripe old age of 91.

I also had to honour a promise made to old friend and local resident, Llew Thomas, featured earlier, who insisted that it was mandatory that I join his local choir, Meibion y Machlud, based in Cowbridge.

This also serves the purpose of keeping my Welsh language a little more alive, in that whilst one hears very little Welsh spoken in Llantwit, this Cowbridge choir is made up mainly of West Walians who have returned to Wales like me after a spell in England. The choir is therefore very much Welsh-speaking, with most pieces also being sung in Welsh.

The choir has a schedule of very casual concerts, although every two years they compete more seriously at the National Eisteddfod when located in South Wales, and have recently been accepted to compete at the Llangollen International Eisteddfod.

Is this not a true immersion in Welshness: singing on stage at national and international eisteddfodau?

Gill has started to produce charity notelets and greetings cards featuring her paintings of St Illtyd's and other designs of hers. They are to be found on sale at the church shop, in aid of church funds, and at various coffee mornings organised by, amongst others, the St Athan Golf Club. And I have kept busy writing and publishing this book in my continued search for Welshness.

How Welsh does one actually feel in Llantwit?

I have made much of the lack of attention the British (i.e. London and English) media give to Wales. In Wales itself one is less conscious of this. I have discovered that the *Sunday Times*, unlike *The Times*, has a Welsh edition, albeit limited to a couple of extra sports pages with an almost patronising Welsh focus. And both the BBC and ITV mainstream TV channels have added a Wales suffix to their logos, with the voice-over between programmes having a Welsh bias, often reminding us of those daily news and current affairs programmes which are directed at a Welsh audience (although coincidentally only broadcast in Wales).

The creation of a more devolved government in Cardiff has however made the interpretation of media articles more complex. Previously the provision of combined statistics for England and Wales had in any case always made it impossible to assess Wales's performance, as this represented such a small proportion of the total. However, with responsibility for such things as health and education now handled separately in Westminster and Cardiff, it is often difficult to discern which

Native printing presses, coupled with the publishing efforts of the London Welsh, energised poets and balladeers, historians and political pamphleteers.'

It has often been said that it takes a period in exile to develop a greater consciousness of one's own nationality. Jon Gower describes how 'Wales helped light up the intellectual life of London and other English cities, and key Welsh figures delved back into the past to establish the tradition, the ancient dignity and identity of the Welsh.'

The Honourable Society of Cymmrodorion was set up in 1751, publishing ancient texts that linked the Welsh to the ancient Britons. This was followed by the forming of the Gwyneddigion Society in 1770 whose advice was in fact sought in 1789 by Thomas Jones of Corwen, beginning the process which eventually led to the first National Eisteddfod in 1861.

There had long been a tradition in the Middle Ages for poetic and musical contests between those of the Welsh bardic order. Poets would compete for a chair at the royal court (hence the name eisteddfod from the Welsh word *eistedd* meaning 'to sit down'). The first such eisteddfod was thought to have been sponsored by Lord Rhys in Cardigan in 1176.

The sixteenth century saw the demise of the bardic order, but the Welsh cultural renaissance of the eighteenth century saw attempts to revive such bardic traditions, initially in the form of poetic assemblies held in taverns. It was then through the efforts of such as Thomas Jones and the Gwyneddigion which saw such contests take the form of much grander popular festivals.

The most vocal of the London Welsh was a stonemason called Edward Williams (Iolo Morganwg) who steadfastly believed that the Welsh were the most important people in the British Isles, and that they could trace an unbroken line back to the druids. Writing in both Welsh and English, he rejoiced in the history of Wales, and in the absence of historical sources he would create his own, helped also by regular doses of the drug laudanum.

15

He created the Gorsedd of Bards (bardic circle) and inaugurated the first bardic circle of stones on Primrose Hill in London in 1792. By 1819 the Gorsedd had become an integral part of the eisteddfod process, with an invitation to join the circle being as significant, to Welshmen, as the Queen's Honours List. Until recently, a year prior to each National Eisteddfod saw a circle of Gorsedd stones erected at the proposed location of the forthcoming eisteddfod. They are therefore to be found in most towns in Wales.

The institutionalisation of Welshness would continue throughout the nineteenth century, so that by 1900 Wales would have a national library, a national museum, university colleges and even a national anthem.

The other significant and parallel occurrence in the development, or lack of development, of Welsh nationhood, was the industrial revolution, post 1750, with the structure of the growing urban industrial settlements imposed by the foreign entrepreneurs mirroring those of Norman and medieval times.

Harold Carter analyses Merthyr Tydfil in 1851. There were three distinct groups in the town. First there was the high-status, English-born population engaged in professional and managerial occupations. It was predominantly Anglican, occupying the High Street. The concept of suburbanisation was to come much later. The exception was the ironmasters in their mansions overlooking their ironworks.

The second group was made up of the skilled and semi-skilled workers in the iron industry. It was essentially Welsh in character, being made up of migrants from rural Wales. It was overwhelmingly nonconformist. They tended to occupy territory adjacent to the various ironworks. Thirdly, there was a group made up of those lowest in the social order, unskilled labourers by occupation, in which the Irish were to form a clear section.

English was the medium of technology and business, and there was also the growth of a clerical class to which many aspired, and for which the English language was also a prerequisite of membership.

Yet even as recently as 1850, Welsh was most people's first language, with the proportion of English speakers in Wales being about 20%, the same as those speaking Welsh today. But then, according to Siôn Jobbins, in his writings for *Cambria* magazine, 'throughout the "long nineteenth century" the British state squeezed the Welsh language out of Wales through the law courts, the new institutions of the county councils, and the notorious "Welsh Not" of the 1870 Education Act.' (The Welsh Not was a piece of wood attached to a rope which was hung around a child's neck if he or she was caught speaking Welsh in the playground. At the end of the day the final recipient of the Not was duly punished. Ironically, it was the Welsh teaching staff who mainly applied such punishment.)

A rationale for this was provided in the pages of the 1847 Government Report on the State of Education in Wales (the infamous 'Treason of the Blue Books'), the formation of which was again encouraged by a Welshman, another William Williams, an MP who was concerned about the inability of his countrymen to speak English.

The report, written by English-speaking Anglicans who disapproved of the Welsh-speaking chapel background of the majority of the Welsh populace, concluded that 'the Welsh language is a vast drawback to the Welsh and a manifold barrier to the moral progress and commercial prosperity of the people. It is not easy to over-estimate its evil effect.' The contents of the report weren't actually digested by the population at large until 1852, as only then was it translated into Welsh.

But this Welsh population was able by dint of numbers to eventually exert an influence. According to Harold Carter, 'the nineteenth century, like the post-medieval period, is marked by the struggle of the people to possess their own cities.'

It, too, was marked by violence (the most well-known episodes were the Merthyr Riot of 1831 and the Newport Rising of the Chartists in 1839, both concerned with the attainment of

Blue Books – written 1847 / translated to Welsh 1852 [handwritten marginal note]

universal male suffrage and the improvement of living standards for all). Change was more rapid, for the Anglo-Normans had been settlers whereas the iron-masters were prepared to move out after fortunes had been made. The apotheosis of change was possibly marked by the Parliamentary elections of 1868.

Carter adds, 'It was confidentially expected that Henry Austin Bruce, later Baron Aberdare, would be returned. He had represented Merthyr since 1852, but he came bottom of the poll, which was topped by Henry Richard.

'...There were three elements in Richard's cause, Welshness, for he conducted most of his meetings in Welsh, nonconformity and working class interests. Here again is the Welsh working people taking over the town and making it in their image. As that happened, the segmentation that had characterised the town slowly disappeared so that by the end of the century it was status which was the discriminator not ethnic identity.'

The intentions of religion and liberalism, eventually socialism, were however played out on a much larger canvas than represented by the need to preserve a Welsh identity. Socialism was international in concept, and nonconformity was about the saving of souls not countries, and also weakened as a movement by the existence of a multitude of different denominations.

Yet it was religion which created the very first statutes which recognised Wales as a separate political entity, namely the Sunday Closing Act of 1881 and the Welsh Church Act of 1914 (implemented in 1920) which disestablished the Anglican Church in Wales, making it the Church in Wales as opposed to the Church of England. And it was Lloyd George and his Liberals who sponsored the Welsh Intermediate Education Act of 1889, which gave counties and boroughs the right to establish intermediate or secondary schools, putting Wales ahead of England when it came to matters of state-sponsored secondary education.

With the growth of the South Wales coalfield and the

working-class demands of its massive labour force, Lloyd George's Liberals gave way to the birth of the Labour Party.

As the dominant political party in the Wales of the twentieth century, its focus was far more on the class struggle than the demands of national identity. But the poverty and poor working conditions of these new major urban centres of population also created communities which, although very different in nature from the rural Wales of old, had similar shared needs, which gave rise to a not-dissimilar sense of community bred out of hardship.

And such communities also developed distinctive personalities, much of which is reflected in the Welsh character of today. Such personality was founded on religion, music and sport.

A century ago Wales was probably one of the most religious countries in the world. Between the mid-eighteenth and mid-nineteenth centuries Wales experienced fifteen major religious revivals, resulting in its reputation as the 'Land of Revivals'. And 1904, aided by a burgeoning media presence, was the biggest of them all. Work in coalmines and metal works would usually begin with a prayer, the favoured leisure activities were communal hymn singing and Bible readings, rugby clubs were disbanded as not being an activity compatible with being a true Christian, and pubs and taverns saw a fall in the consumption of the demon drink.

There were up to 150 chapels in the Rhondda Valleys by the end of the nineteenth century, with room for congregations up to 2,000 strong.

The nonconformist religion both helped and hindered the cause of Welsh nationalism. Like socialism, they were fighting a far greater cause than the needs of a Welsh identity. With the disestablishment of the Anglican Church in Wales, and the greater promotion of the Welsh language, the chapels encouraged people to think of Wales as an independent entity, but their encouragement of the Welsh language was not an end in itself, it was the means by which Christianity could prosper.

To again quote Siôn Jobbins: 'To read the Welsh press of

Welsh Press ?? [handwritten annotation]

the nineteenth century is to be struck with the importance of religion in Welsh life. This was the one subject that exercised Welsh minds and milked the country's intellectual energy, much to the detriment of our language and national development. Rather than saving the language, the Sunday school acted as an educational ghetto, diverting energy from campaigning against the Welsh Not.'

And: 'The campaign for the disestablishment of the Church sapped generations of Welsh political leaders. They, and the anti-alcohol campaigns, were the only Welsh political results of religious difference. There was no mass language campaign: Welsh nonconformism was a pliant accomplice in the slow death of the Welsh language, not its saviour.'

But with such large numbers in every congregation, the music as well as the language of religion must have created a big impact, helped by the tonic sol-fa movement which made it more accessible to the untrained population. In addition, eisteddfodau, celebrations of the twin Welsh heritage of poetry and music, ensured that singing also contributed to the general sense of community and unity. In fact hymn-singing festivals used to draw crowds of thousands, even in excess of sporting fixtures. Writes Jon Gower, 'in 1893, when Wales won rugby's Triple Crown for the first time, they beat England in front of a crowd of 15,000; the same year there were 20,000 people enjoying the chief choral competitions at the National Eisteddfod, held that year in Pontypridd.'

But sport also had a big part to play. John Davies writes in his *A History of Wales* that at the beginning of the last century, 'the rugby clubs could draw upon the strong tradition of communal activity which had taken root in the industrial districts of Wales', and that 'as Gareth Williams and Dai Smith argue, the more energetic the physical labour in which a workforce is involved, the more strenuous the physical relief it craves.'

John Davies continues, 'With the formation of the WRU in 1881, the union's principal founder, Richard Mullock of

Newport, wanted a national rather than a provincial team, and as a result rugby was grafted on to Welshness and became a powerful symbol of the nation's identity.'

The period 1900–1914 was the first golden age of Welsh rugby, with Wales winning the Triple Crown six times in twelve years, plus three Grand Slams with France beginning to join in European competition, and the defeats of the touring New Zealand All Blacks and Australian Wallabies (although not the South Africans).

'And full employment,' writes Jon Gower, 'gave everyone something to sing about. When the age of coal began, Welsh morale was at rock bottom, yet by the end of the nineteenth century the Welsh were seen as an upright and honest people. And the South Wales coal boom was one of the principal causes of change.'

But whereas the earlier part of the industrial revolution in Wales had seen a major movement of population from rural areas to provide the required industrial labour, the early years of the twentieth century saw much more widespread immigration into Wales, from Ireland, from the west of England (Gwyn Nicholls, the prince of Welsh rugby three-quarters, was actually born in Gloucestershire) and further afield from countries like Italy. Across the whole of the globe, only the USA saw a higher level of immigration.

Population growth saw the greatest ever number of Welsh speakers, but with English still being the language of business and government, and a growing number of immigrants, the industrial valleys of South Wales became gradually anglicised. The percentage of the population speaking Welsh dropped from 50% in 1900 to only 19% in 1990.

Alun Richards, a Welsh author born in 1929, talked about Welsh becoming his 'grandmother's language' with a 'special Sundays-only' significance, quoting another English-language Welsh author, Gwyn Thomas's words, who described Welsh as having 'the status of a pet, reserved for occasional greetings.'

This was all during a period when economically the good

times were also at an end. The first fifty years of the century would see a major worldwide depression in the 1930s plus the cataclysmic effect of two world wars. The latter, whilst causing so much hardship and death, would also serve to reduce the number of Welsh speakers, and make the population in general feel more British in support of the common cause.

And the Welsh people, persuaded to believe in the superiority of all things English, became complicit in their own demise. With the growth in the 1950s of radio and television ownership, half of the households in Wales were by 1959 paying for a TV licence, even without a corresponding growth in broadcasting from Wales, either in Welsh or English. Writes Siôn Jobbins in *Cambria* magazine, 'There was even suspicion towards a Welsh broadcasting service... with some Labour MPs such as George Thomas complaining that the BBC in Wales was "corrupting the minds of the Welsh people" with what was seen as a Welsh nationalist bias – a rather incredible assertion, unless any broadcasting through the medium of Welsh, or nod to Welsh nationality, was assumed to be nationalistic propaganda.'

The Welsh Labour Party have always put socialism before nationalism, continually putting themselves in conflict with an equally left-wing Plaid Cymru.

Yet the socialists also failed in their industrial ambitions. The latter half of the twentieth century saw the final and complete demise of the heavy industry on which South Wales had become totally dependent. In 1913 the coal industry was Wales's largest employer, accounting for over a quarter of the male labour force. South Wales produced 20% of the UK's coal output and 30% of coal exports. Cardiff was the largest coal exporting port in the world. All that now remains are a few drift and open-cast mines, plus one small deep mine. The last large deep mine, Tower Colliery, having been run as a miners' co-operative since 1994, finally closed in 2008. The removal of the coal mines has proved to be a body blow to the Welsh economy and the livelihood of its people.

The word of God would also become increasingly challenged. With far greater mobility of population, and the growth of mass media, people would become less dependent on religion to create a heart for local communities, and less enthused about the 'Bible black', dour nonconformist image, incorporating, as it did in Wales until the end of the twentieth century, the concept of 'Sunday closing'.

In parallel with this economic and religious decline, a minority – a mainly Welsh-speaking minority – have nevertheless successfully managed to make their views heard and respected over the last fifty years. This minority, claims Harold Carter in *Against the Odds*, were essentially a new Welsh bourgeoisie who operated social and health services, and the increasingly complex system of government in Wales that followed the creation of the Welsh Office in 1964.

Organisations such as Plaid Cymru, the Party of Wales, and *Cymdeithas yr Iaith Gymraeg*, the Welsh Language Society, have also, through mainly peaceful protest, seen the Welsh language achieve official status alongside English, at least in government if not in business, along with the teaching of the language as compulsory in schools up to the age of sixteen, the launch of a Welsh language TV channel, and finally, the birth of a Welsh National Assembly in 1999.

Much of the support for such momentous achievements was achieved partly as a reaction to events which clearly showed the lack of interest and concern that Westminster had for the needs and views of the Welsh people. I speak of the massive Welsh protest, incorporating many prominent Welsh personalities, all the local authorities and all but one of the Welsh MPs, generated in 1965 by the drowning of the Tryweryn Valley and the farming community of Capel Celyn to supply water to the city of Liverpool. I speak of the mining disaster of Aberfan in 1966, when a waterlogged coal tip engulfed a total of 144 people, including 116 children, and the failure of the National Coal Board to admit its responsibility for the tragedy, and the later outrageous decision by a Labour government to raid the public donations to the Disaster Fund to help pay for the removal of the tips.

And for Welsh miners and politicians, the miners' strike of the 1980s became as much a struggle about nationhood as industrial politics. The closing of the coal mines was a body blow to the Welsh economy and the livelihood of its people. But Maggie Thatcher was 'not for turning'.

She did turn, however, in response to Gwynfor Evans's threatened hunger strike if the government failed to approve the introduction of the Welsh language TV channel, S4C.

And the Welsh people finally gave their approval in 1999 to a Welsh National Assembly – just – by a majority of 6,721, or 0.6% of those who voted.

But, in the words of journalist Martin Shipton, the Assembly is a 'Poor Man's Parliament'. Anti-devolutionists within the Welsh Labour Party manoeuvred behind the scenes to ensure the proposed Assembly would not have the ability to pass its own laws. It took another 12 years of debating the legislative process, rather than concentrating on the political matters in hand, plus the insistence on a referendum in 2011, to permit such powers. And, until the Wales Act 2017, they still only existed in specific areas such as education and health, and until 2019 will exist without the additional facility to levy the taxes required to fund the policies proposed.

Is it any wonder that the Assembly has struggled to produce sensible policies for its electorate? But this is also a consequence of the Welsh being their own worst enemy as well as intransigence at Westminster.

The Welsh love of committees has tended to produce an over-bureaucratic structure with excessive levels of government for such a small region.

And, to again quote Martin Shipton, 'only in Wales would the shortcomings of politicians be cited as a reason to abolish the democratic national body to which they have been elected. No one, so far as I am aware, advocated the abolition of the

House of Commons in the wake of the MPs' expenses scandal of 2009.'

So Wales is still not a nation nor even a federal state. Yet the population sees itself as Welsh, not British nor English.

As mentioned earlier, in the 2001 Census, the choice of 'Welsh' was typically omitted from a question relating to perceived national identity. Instead Harold Carter references a study, also published in 2001, by the Centre for Research into Elections and Social Trends which is presented in a paper by Robert Anderson entitled 'National identity and independence attitudes: minority nationalism in Scotland and Wales.' The study was based on the returns from a random sample of some 1,255 people aged over eighteen conducted partly by phone and partly by post. Respondents were asked to classify themselves as Welsh or British based on what the author calls the 'Moreno scale'. The answers to the question 'Which of the following best describes how you see yourself?' were as follows:

Welsh not British	18%
More Welsh than British	20%
Equally Welsh and British	39%
More British than Welsh	8%
British not Welsh	15%

Despite a total lack of political or geographical integrity, the vast majority of the population saw themselves as Welsh, with almost half of this majority seeing themselves as more Welsh than British.

For the 2011 Census, Welsh, for the first time, was included alongside English and British as an option in a list of identities from which respondents could make a multiple choice.

These results were even more positive. Sixty-six% of residents considered themselves Welsh, with 58% singularly so, and only 7% also ticking British. And when one adds the fact that 27% of census respondents were born outside of Wales, it means that practically all 'Welsh nationals' identify themselves, first and foremost, as Welsh.

So what makes them Welsh? What characteristics have we gleaned from this short pocket history of Wales that identifies what it is to be Welsh; to be from Wales?

Language and Culture

The obvious first ingredient is the presence of a different, unique language. Until the beginning of the last century almost half the people living in the land known as Wales spoke Welsh and not English. The Acts of Union of 1536 and 1542 had made it difficult for Welshmen to hold public office, and insisted that English be the language of business and government, but the peasantry working in the fields, *y werin*, persisted in living their lives, their work and their culture, through their native tongue, whilst the Church also educated them in the Welsh language.

Following the 'Treason of the Blue Books' in 1847, formal education had to be taught through the medium of English, and the Industrial Revolution saw wholesale immigration of English speakers into the new urban Wales. So the twentieth century almost saw the demise of the Welsh language, with only one in five of the population now speaking it. But the efforts of the Welsh-speaking minority in the latter half of the century eventually saw Welsh accepted as an official language in the Welsh Language Act of 1993 and Welsh being taught in all schools up to the age of 16. A first independent Welsh-medium primary school was actually created in 1939 in Aberystwyth, with the first local authority school opening in Llanelli in 1947, followed by a nursery in Maesteg in 1949, and a secondary school in Rhyl in 1956. Degree courses were taught in Welsh in Aberystwyth and Bangor from the 1960s. There are now 464 primary and 55 secondary Welsh-medium schools, and even in Cardiff, 12% of primary school pupils are now taught in Welsh. The capital city is not situated in a particularly Welsh-speaking part of Wales, but since its development as the centre of Welsh media and government, it has attracted a growing number of Welsh speakers.

But a century of parallel anglicisation has produced a divided society. For much of the twentieth century, little Welsh language or history was taught in schools. First-language Welsh speakers spoke Welsh in the playground, but English in the classroom.

And then with Welsh becoming compulsory in the classroom the non-Welsh speakers also felt ostracised. One such non-Welsh speaker, Alun Richards, quoted earlier, wrote: 'It is a difficult thing to explain to an outsider how a man can feel a stranger in his own country, and the indifference of many Welshmen to their nation springs from the feeling, often justified, of being excluded where executive positions are reserved for those with bilingual qualifications.'

And whilst Welsh has become compulsory in the classroom, English has become the language of the playground and Facebook, encouraged by the globalisation created by both mass and social media.

However there is no credence to the argument that the efforts to promote the Welsh language are misplaced because they work on behalf of a mere 20% minority. Such promotion is totally acceptable purely as a matter of democracy. Every minority have an unquestioned right to preserve their language and culture. And there are plenty of examples of regions of the globe where different languages are able to exist side by side. In California, Spanish has status alongside English; Canada has French speaking provinces. And even minor languages can achieve acceptance. Flemish is spoken by a majority of Belgians. The minority language in Switzerland, Romansh, has some official status within a small area of the country.

Professor T J Morgan of Swansea University once wrote: 'The urge to survive does not depend upon arguments and evidence for its justification; the desire is its own justification. The concept of survival can be applied to the language, for in the make-up of many of us the language is an extension of ourselves.'

And there are signs that even the non-speaking Welsh are

recognising the need to persevere with the language. In an opinion poll carried out for the Welsh Language Board in 1996, 96% of speakers and an almost-as-high 94% of non-Welsh speakers agreed that the number of Welsh speakers should increase. And a report by Beaufort Research in the summer of 2013 found that 99% of respondents who didn't speak much Welsh said that they would like to be able to speak Welsh better than they did, and 92% would welcome more opportunities to speak Welsh.

To quote Harold Carter, 'the strength of language is as a carrier of historical and cultural associations.' And Ned Thomas, writing in *The Welsh Extremist*, adds: 'By its existence, the language tells us we are Welsh. All the feelings of nationality that are supported for Englishmen by the Queen, the Houses of Parliament, London policemen, bewigged judges, and a whole range of political, cultural and popular institutions rest for the Welshman on the language and literature.'

For example, how do you translate words like *hwyl* and *hiraeth* into English? And for me, one of the lasting benefits of the fifty years of pressure by Cymdaethas yr Iaith Gymraeg is bilingual road signs. They clearly state that you are now not in England, but actually in Wales. To hell with any cost, they are a definitive statement of our identity.

And singing hymns in Welsh is decidedly more moving than singing them in English. Whatever the merits of Shakespeare's language, Welsh feels far more suited to the demands of religious passion and fervour, even if, as a non-Welsh speaking Welshman, I can't understand a word I am singing.

Music in fact is another element of our culture which defines our Welshness. As already mentioned, there has long been a tradition in Wales for poetic and musical competition, which came to full fruition with the birth of the modern eisteddfod in the middle of the nineteenth century.

Initially modern eisteddfodau focussed mainly on song, and the choral competitions attracted huge crowds, even at smaller local eisteddfodau. Most popular amongst the songs was *Hen*

Wlad Fy Nhadau, composed in 1856 by Pontypridd father and son Evan and James James, soon to be adopted as an unofficial Welsh national anthem. And writes Jon Gower, 'over the course of some thirty years, inspirational conductors such as Griffith Rhys Jones, better known as Caradog, whipped novice singers into single musical entities, able to tackle even the most ornate and complicated works, and garner fame throughout the UK. He led the South Wales Choral Union, which beat allcomers at the Crystal Palace two years running, a crucial moment in the creation of a choral nation.'

Jon Gower even goes on to suggest that it was Caradog who originally coined the description of Wales as the 'Land of Song'.

I recall taking my mother to a local Llanelli pub for Sunday lunch, to be sat next to a large farming family gathering who burst into song, singing hymns between each food course.

And when my wife and I attended a St David's Day celebration sponsored by the London Welsh Rugby Supporters Club, my wife, who hails from Essex, remarked that it was the first formal dinner dance function she had attended when the dancing was preceded by hymn singing over the coffee.

Most of us can manage to sing a Welsh hymn or two, even if the words are uttered phonetically with zero understanding of their meaning.

The modern day eisteddfod also offers far more than song, encompassing drama, arts, crafts, architecture, dance, and even a blossoming pop music scene centred on Maes B, a second eisteddfod 'field' aimed specifically at the young. Although surprisingly it is only latterly that the eisteddfod has openly attempted to contribute to the preservation of the Welsh language, with a 'Welsh-only' rule being introduced as recently as 1950 at Caerffili (Caerphilly).

As well as a National Eisteddfod we also now have the Llangollen International Eisteddfod (acclaimed worldwide, although largely ignored by the BBC), and a youth eisteddfod organised under the auspices of Urdd Gobaith Cymru (the

Welsh League of Youth), an organisation founded in 1922 and now the world's largest youth movement with 1,500 branches and 50,000 members.

The ultimate Welshman, rugby hero, broadcaster and actor, Ray Gravell, had this to say about the Urdd: 'Over the years, I realised the importance of the movement to modern Wales, especially in terms of entertainment aimed at young people. It was at the Urdd camps that the fledgling Welsh pop scene developed from the Sixties onwards, and the camps also gave many young people who were non-Welsh speakers the opportunity to use the language for the first time. We'd be a much poorer country without the activities that happen in these centres, and that is also true about the Urdd Eisteddfod. Where else in the world would you see tens of thousands of children practising for months to recite and sing and dance at their *eisteddfod gylch*?'

Community

Another endearing quality of Welshness is our sense of community. This could, in the days of religious puritan fervour, be narrow and limiting, but in general it generates warmth, equality and a sense of fair play (or as Welsh speakers frequently say, *chwarae teg*).

I earlier referenced J Geraint Jenkins's paper on 'Life and Traditions in Rural Wales' which spoke of the co-operation and hospitality that characterised society in medieval Wales, and the focus of its legal system on reconciliation, common sense and respect.

George Monbiot, writing in *The Guardian*, echoes such thoughts with reference to today's society, and talks of being told by Elfyn Llwyd, ex-Plaid Cymru MP for Dwyfor Meirionnydd, of a local farm whose tenants were about to be evicted because the farmer had been killed in an accident. The neighbouring farmers clubbed together and told the landlord they would look after the husbandry until the oldest boy turned eighteen.

Elfyd Llwyd concluded: 'Perhaps it's a result of living in a sparsely populated area. We help each other because we know each other... Traditionally Welsh people belong to the left. There's a deep and ingrained sense of fair play. They want to see people being looked after. The University of Bangor was built on donations from quarrymen earning a pittance, because they wanted a better future for their children.'

This community spirit found in rural Wales we also saw resurfacing in the South Wales mining communities created by the Industrial Revolution and the growth of the South Wales coalfield.

Returning Welsh exile, Cledwyn Davies, whose story is featured later in the book, talks about three years spent in the mining village of Llantwit Vardre: 'With houses on top of each other, this was a close valley community with very much its own camaraderie, even its own dialect.'

Various members of Plaid Cymru also speak of their pride in what is both their birthplace and their current residence:

'To me the Valleys have so much going for them. I feel privileged to live in a place so enriched with history, culture and a deep sense of community spirit. I was born and brought up in the Rhondda. I live on the same street in Penygraig where I was raised as a child and my seven-year-old daughter is growing up in the security that comes from people living close together in a strong community. For me, it's the people that makes the Valleys special and what they make is something that money cannot buy.' (Leanne Wood, leader of Plaid Cymru).

'The Valleys are my home, and if I won the lottery, I wouldn't want to live anywhere else. I have always lived in the Valleys around Caerphilly and this is truly where I belong. My family and friends all live locally, and the vibrancy of the community makes this a wonderful place to be. What I appreciate most... is the friendliness of the community – here are people who genuinely do look out for their neighbours, family, friends or even strangers.' (Lindsay Whittle, Plaid Cymru AM for Caerphilly in South Wales East region, until 2016).

'For me, the Valleys are its unrivalled natural beauty and its people. The ordinary people who still hold the fondly-held values of being a good neighbour, of caring and of living life with an unassuming dignity.' (Jocelyn Davies, Plaid Cymru regional AM, South Wales East, until 2016).

George Monbiot, an English author now living in Wales, observes in *The Guardian* that over two years of walking through the valleys and over the hills, he had come 'to form the impression that Wales is less socially stratified, less grasping, more liberal than the rest of Britain.'

And these thoughts are echoed by Welsh travel writer, Jan Morris, who states in her book *Wales: Epic Views of a Small Country* that 'it was not simply romanticising to claim, even in 1997, that in many parts of Wales a particular kind of society still flourished in a way generally forgotten elsewhere. A relationship almost familial, still bound friends, neighbours and even opponents. Class meant far less than it did in England, and sect had become almost irrelevant.'

Y Wlad/The Land

The warmth for Wales and the Valleys felt by the various Plaid Cymru parliamentarians quoted above is not only generated by a love of the people, but also by a love of the land itself, its beauty and grandeur.

'The rugged landscape framing almost every village and town gives us an abundance of beautiful scenery.' (Leanne Wood, leader of Plaid Cymru)

'The best thing about growing up in the Cynon Valley was the freedom we had to explore because of the fantastic countryside, and the safety that came from always knowing that someone was looking out for you.' (Rhuanedd Richards, ex-chief executive, Plaid Cymru).

And to repeat part of an earlier quote: 'For me, the Valleys are its unrivalled natural beauty and its people.' (Jocelyn Davies, Plaid Cymru regional AM for South Wales East until 2016).

We should not undervalue the loveliness of our landscape, yet not broadcast it too much for fear of attracting too many English visitors and potential residents. This landscape was part of the reason for many of the returning exiles I feature later in the book deciding to relocate to Wales. And it was also a major feature in encouraging the non-Welsh partners of these exiles to go along with their move.

A good way to illustrate the hold that Wales as a land can have on people is to quote the views of foreigners who became transfixed almost from their first exposure.

American Pamela Petro studied Welsh in Lampeter, claiming that 'the desire to learn Welsh is all about place. I can't imagine wanting to learn Welsh without knowing Wales.' But finding it too easy in Wales to fall back into speaking English, to improve her Welsh she travelled the world looking for non-English speaking Welsh speakers, providing a chronicle of her journey in her fascinating book *Travels in an Old Tongue*.

Imogen Rhia Herrad was born and grew up in Germany, and apparently like many of her compatriots had a fascination for all things Celtic. She planned a year in Britain as a foreign language assistant and chose rural Wales as a location. Within the space of a week she had 'fallen utterly in love with the place', claiming that 'there was something about the grandiose beauty of the mountains that sent shivers down her spine.'

And for Imogen the language worked hand-in-hand with the landscape to create almost a sense of physical mystery. She became 'fascinated by the weirdly-spelt place names on bilingual signposts. Could there really be a place called Llwchwr? These names seemed to betoken the presence of not just another language, but a whole other layer of reality. There seemed to be a mystery about Welsh somehow, in this small land beyond England, beyond the mountains.'

Imogen next went in search of the Welsh in Patagonia and developed an even greater fascination with the environment and the struggles of the original natives of this far-off land, so strange to a European perspective. She tells the story of her time in Wales and Patagonia in her book: *Beyond the Pampas: In Search of Patagonia.*

Finally there is Heinke, also German, once a fellow Welsh learner with me at classes in the London Welsh Centre in London's Kings Cross. Working at the time as a surgical registrar across various London hospitals, she had preceded this with a spell performing a similar function at Morriston Hospital, Swansea.

She has not been unhappy in London, and she enjoyed previous times spent in South Africa, Scotland and Liverpool. But Wales was different. 'I like the people, of course. They'll chat to anybody. And it's smaller: everyone knows each other: it's the old Welsh village thing. But it's the continuous, imposing presence of the country. I feel closer to the land. It's really quite strange. I love the countryside, going for walks, the history, the sights. My feelings are deeper.'

Rugby

Former Welsh First Minister, the late Rhodri Morgan, once said that 'in Wales what is special is small-country psychology – a special kind of need for heroes that could reassure us of our existence as a country.'

Such an identity can also be created through sport. Unlike the Catalans and the Basques, the Welsh, Scottish and Irish can express their nationality through their sporting teams. And the foremost of these for Wales is their rugby union team.

Every Welsh exile I have interviewed for my books, whether Welsh-speaking or not, whether Welsh-born or first generation, spoke of all their offspring, even grandchildren, being ardent Welsh rugby fans. I am willing to bet that every man, boy, woman or girl from the families I interviewed is the proud possessor of a Welsh rugby shirt. Wearing a Welsh rugby shirt is a clear visible sign announcing that you are Welsh.

Ironically, and sadly, the Welsh jersey's iconic national symbol is a very English Prince of Wales feathers, supported by a German motto.

The one major absentee from this exiles fan club of Welsh rugby is my own daughter. In protest at the way I nurtured my son as a Wales and Scarlets supporter, my daughter's rugby allegiance is England first, Ireland second (her mother is first generation Irish), and Wales not at all. I even had to buy her an England rugby shirt to celebrate England's return to Grand Slam winning ways in the early 1990s.

But Welsh rugby is more than just a team to support. Roger Lewis, Welsh rugby's ex-CEO, announced his mission with the words, 'the WRU will take Wales to the world and, in our stadium, will welcome the world to Wales. Together we will play our part in defining Wales as a nation.'

To quote Owen Sheers, recently the WRU's artist in residence, 'there are moments in history when a nation becomes a stadium. When a country's gaze and speech tightens in one direction.'

And world expert on biomechanics, Frans Bosch, whilst acting as a physical training specialist to the WRU, warmed to the 'family coherence' of the Wales rugby set-up: 'I went to watch a match in Cardiff, and I realised I was seeing the country, not a sport. A cultural event, not a game.'

And even an Englishman, former international Paul Ackford, stated in *The Times* that, 'Of all the international grounds, the Millennium (now the Principality) Stadium is by far the most atmospheric and evocative, and the Welsh crowd the most inspirational. Despite Stuart Lancaster's laudable attempts to invest Twickenham with some vigour and reaction, it is Cardiff that exhibits the strongest, most genuine connection between a country, a sport and a team. More expressive than New Zealanders, who can be a touch dour, the French, who can be temperamental, and the South Africans, who can be a touch arrogant, the Welsh are the real deal, and it is uplifting to be there when they give voice to their passion.'

Football is actually more popular than rugby in Wales, in that there are more Welshmen playing and watching football than rugby on a regular basis. And Wales has suddenly come alive at national level, with its major success of reaching the semi-finals of Euro 2016, and at club level, with Swansea and Cardiff City doing rather well over the last six or more years. But crucially over time we have been far more successful at rugby. For a country with a mere three million population, to compete on equal terms with a fifty million-plus neighbour across the course of more than 100 games has to be a major achievement. It has, however, to be admitted that New Zealand has achieved far more with a not much larger four-and-a-half million people; and we won't mention Samoa with its population of just 200,000!

But since Welsh rugby's so-called first Golden Era at the start of the last century, the mood of the Welsh people has seemed indomitably linked to the success or otherwise of the Welsh rugby team. This could merely be a reflection of the fact that the ebb and flow of the fortunes of Welsh rugby seemed to match the state of the economy. In times of recession and depression, Welsh rugby always seemed to suffer. Perhaps a failing economy actually had a direct effect on the size and demeanour of the crowds, and the manner in which the team performed. In the pre- professional era it also increased the likelihood of star players succumbing to the monetary delights of the devil that was rugby league. Now that rugby union has also become professional, Welsh rugby has a more major challenge to succeed without the funding and television revenues available to English and French clubs.

To quote Alan Phillips, Wales's team manager: 'It's either the wedding game or the funeral game with us.'

Yet Welsh rugby has achieved such an iconic status, it is even suggested in jest that its influence extends well beyond the boundaries of Wales itself. A particularly spurious statistical connection was explored in a festive Christmas edition of none other than the British Medical Journal. The BMJ investigated the urban myth that 'every time Wales win the rugby Grand Slam, a Roman Catholic Pope dies, except in 1978 when Wales were really good, and two Popes died.'

The report concluded that, 'there is no evidence of a link

between papal deaths and any home nation Grand Slam…' but that 'there was, however, weak statistical evidence to support an association between Welsh performance and the number of papal deaths.' Written in 2008, it recommended that 'given the dominant Welsh performance of 2008, the Vatican medical team should take special care of the pontiff this Christmas.'

There are, however, those who claim that supporters of the Welsh rugby team are only really concerned about beating the English. Just as, historically, the innate socialism of the Welsh only became radicalism when the establishment in Westminster was seen as the enemy, so does the Welsh rugby performance go up a notch only when confronting the English. Our mediocre record against the southern hemisphere giants bears testimony to this.

Travel writer, Jan Morris, observed in her book *Wales: Epic Views of a Small Country* that 'the Welsh have seldom suffered from national ambition, only national grievance.'

Take away the common enemy and we descend into tribalism. The true rugby supporter in Wales itself has always actually cared more about his local team than the national side.

As a Scarlet, 'a Scarlet till I die', it is a matter of conjecture as to whether a Scarlet European cup success or a Welsh World Cup would be seen as the greater triumph.

Swansea people disdainfully call us Turks; we call them Jacks. On holiday in 1997, following the British and Irish Lions in South Africa, I was bought a drink by a Swansea supporter, who protested bitterly that 'he hadn't travelled 5,000 miles just to buy a bloody Turk a drink.'

Until the end of the 1960s the Welsh rugby team was selected by a committee known as the Big Five, with its personnel split between East and West Wales. When a team was picked to play Australia in 1966, the big debate was not about how best Wales could achieve victory but who should play at fly half: Barry John of Llanelli in West Wales or David Watkins of Newport and East Wales. The result was an irrelevancy. In the event Wales lost for the first time to Australia – that is until the

Waratah's (New South Wales) victory over Wales in 1927 was retrospectively identified as a triumph for Australia itself.

The Welsh Rugby Union, in creating the current four-region structure, have at their peril completely ignored this tribalism. It is one thing to establish a rugby franchise in virgin rugby territory such as Perth in Western Australia, or by London Welsh in Oxford at the Kassam Stadium for that matter, but to impose manufactured regional identities onto geographical areas incorporating many well-established clubs that date back more than 100 years could well be rugby suicide.

Support for the Welsh national team is currently buoyant, but far fewer Welshmen are playing or watching regional or club rugby week in and week out. To survive as part of our culture, irrespective of being a major part of our national identity, Welsh rugby needs its tribalism as much as its hatred of the English.

Attitude of Heart and Mind

Much of the desire to announce our Welshness does stem from a need to be heard, buried as we are beneath a veritable tonnage of Englishness. Actor Matthew Rhys, interviewed in *The Times*, claims that 'Welshmen are raised to shout louder. We're often viewed as the poor or more embarrassing cousin, so that breeds a great passion and patriotism.'

We also have a desire to preserve our friendly provinciality in contrast to the status-driven English.

Yet, until the last fifty years, nationhood itself was not something that bothered the majority of the population of Wales.

American Pamela Petro paints a more abstract picture of what it means to be Welsh: 'Welshness has been a secular construction, consciously fashioned by English and Welsh speakers alike, out of song, grit, pride in origins however humble, a profound respect for difference, and beer. Add to that a streak of wounded defiance directed more practically at the English (*sic*) government, plus an unrefined and unapologetic joy in anything the least bit interesting.'

And travel writer, Jan Morris, believes it is something even deeper: 'Wales... is not just a country on the map, or even in the mind; it is a country of the heart. And all of us have some small country there.'

In Search of Welshness

ON HOLIDAY IN Anglesey with golfing friends from Essex, our group attended a concert given by a local male voice choir. As is the usual custom, to complete the evening, the audience were invited to stand and join the choir in the singing of *Mae Hen Wlad Fy Nhadau*. My Essex friend in the next seat turned to me and said, 'I didn't realise Wales had its own national anthem.'

Llanelli writer Jon Gower, in an article entitled 'English is a Welsh Language: Television's Crisis in Wales' (IWA, 2009), observed that: 'An American writer once suggested that a people that doesn't see itself on television begins to believe it doesn't exist. From a Welsh perspective, if one had to depend on UK network television for a sense of self or, let's go further, a sense of being, there would be ample room for self-doubt and anxiety. It can sometimes seem as if a mantle of invisibility has been cast over us.'

As a Welsh exile living near London, capital not just of England but of the whole UK, I am constantly annoyed, boring my wife in the process, that the so-called British media choose to ignore our very existence. I am also angry that there is little Welsh media, even in Wales itself, and that to watch BBC Wales or S4C in England I have had to become a Sky subscriber.

To unburden myself of this chip on my shoulder, I felt the need to announce and explore my Welshness. As Matthew Rhys puts it, 'Welshmen are raised to shout louder'. So, sitting at home one day, bored with retirement, I started to write down my thoughts and reminiscences of my childhood in Llanelli, and of my adult life in and around London, using these experiences to paint a human and hopefully humorous picture of how the Welsh are different from the English, and also to make a more serious comment about the challenges we face in preserving our identity in an English, or at least, London-dominated world.

I also added short biographies of eight other Welsh exiles, fellow London Welsh rugby supporters at Old Deer Park, and fellow Welsh language learners at the London Welsh Centre in Gray's Inn Road, to explore whether the views of other members of the diaspora were similar to mine.

The resulting book, *In Search of Welshness*, was published in August 2011.

In the 1950s half the population of the Llanelli area spoke Welsh, and even those of us who couldn't became used to singing hymns in Welsh and listening to visiting Welsh preachers droning on at school assemblies, despite having little idea as to what the preacher was saying or what we were singing.

Whilst my father was fluent in Welsh, my mother's family hailed originally from Pembrokeshire, 'little England beyond Wales', so she didn't inherit the Welsh language from her own parents. Most Welsh speakers in Llanelli in fact came from the outlying villages rather than from the town itself, and at school these Welsh speakers were segregated into separate classes from the non-Welsh speakers.

The Welsh language was also not a compulsory school subject, and when forced to make a choice for O-levels, Latin, French and German were often chosen in preference – this despite our Welsh teacher providing us, immediately prior to the day of decision, with the incentive of dramatically improved exam results, with marks in excess of 90%, when 50% had previously been the norm.

Latin, according to my mother, was 'the foundation of all other languages', and French and German were considered to be of far more cultural and commercial use than Welsh in the wider world outside Wales. English was the everyday language of business and government, even amongst Welsh speakers, and in the aftermath of the Second World War there was also a strong focus on being British rather than Welsh. In our family, the Queen's speech was a must-watch event on Christmas Day.

The result of all this was that, in general everyday life, my friends and I conversed almost totally through the medium of English, even though that everyday life still embodied many of the elements of community, music, rugby and a sense of *chwarae teg* (fair play) that I have earlier outlined as being part of the essence of 'Welshness'.

The southern Welsh, partly to escape their industrial background of working in coal and steel, were also always concerned with 'getting on', although for most this meant getting an education rather than becoming millionaires.

This concept of 'getting on' in life also meant, for many of us, the need to leave Llanelli, initially to attend college or university, and subsequently to seek out more worthwhile employment than the area, and possibly Wales, could provide.

Byron Rogers, in his book *Three Journeys*, encountered the same inclinations in the even more anglicised county town of Carmarthen.

'It is very sad. While it was a great town to be brought up in, one always assumed one would leave. To be born in Carmarthen was to await exile... The grammar school had an enormous impact on the town from the late nineteenth century on, but it was an export agency... of my class of thirty at the grammar school, only three now live in the town'.

In addition, in Wales as a whole, there was on the one hand a sense of claustrophobia brought on by the narrowness of a chapel-dominated culture. To quote Byron Rogers, 'the society of West Wales was one soaked in the Bible'. And on the other hand there was very little live modern entertainment or so-called 'culture', popular or otherwise, at least if you were a non-Welsh speaking Welshman. One, therefore, also left Wales to experience the wider world, including the world of London about which the British media persistently told us so much.

Growing up in Wales in the 1950s, we felt a definite pride in being Welsh, but we had no vision of a possible Welsh nation state; Plaid Cymru were 'extremists', equated by my 'true blue' father with communism. The speaking of the Welsh language was not encouraged, and the Welsh Language Society (*Cymdeithas yr Iaith Gymraeg*) was seen as equally extreme, defending their minority rights rather than opening the door to non-Welsh speakers. The British media, in content and in its structure, failed to recognise the actual existence of Wales as an entity, and popular culture radiated from London.

In my own case, it was the move to London which actually raised my consciousness both of my own Welshness and of the disregard for Wales held by British institutions. Well-known Welsh author and academic Ned Thomas quotes Emrys ap Iwan from the nineteenth century, as claiming that spending some time abroad, or with a foreign literature, was a way of making a Welshman more conscious of his own identity. It helped him separate out what in his own background was distinct from English culture. Education and travel do not make Welshmen less concerned with their own history, but more aware of it.

John Davies in his *A History of Wales* commented that, 'By the 1860s, there are indications that some at least among the Welsh saw political implications in their cultural allegiance. This was most obvious among those who had experience outside Wales, in particular in the United States and on Merseyside, the places in which the Patagonia venture had originated.'.

Saunders Lewis, one of the founders of Plaid Cymru, was also born and educated not in Wales but on Merseyside.

I often wonder, if I had stayed in Wales, whether I would have become as concerned about the preservation of Welsh culture and language; whether I would have bothered to join a choir and attempted to relearn the Welsh language.

Are the Welsh who now live in Wales as conscious as I am of the complete disregard of the British media for things Welsh? Their version of the BBC and ITV carries a clear Welsh logo, and will more noticeably highlight Welsh programming, even if there is still very little of it. S4C is obviously more apparent, and they don't have to subscribe to Sky to receive it. It is true that there are no Welsh editions of the national dailies, and the only daily paper published in Wales, the *Western Mail*, is

43

disparagingly referred to as the 'Western Fail', with rumours that its declining circulation might even force it to become a weekly. But we now abide in the era of the internet, and the BBC and the *Western Mail*'s WalesOnline websites, amongst others, offer not only news about Wales but easily accessible Welsh 'regional' news coverage, although with this coverage being provided under the single Trinity Mirror umbrella, it is undoubtedly less diverse than the once-vibrant local-newspaper scene in Wales.

And finally, word of mouth must contribute massively to a sense of belonging and differentiation, and the Welsh are quite good at that. And it's a much more appropriate word of mouth. The inhabitants of Wales don't have to suffer going into the local pub and being asked, 'How are England doing in the Olympics today?'

Perhaps those living in Wales today have no reason to go 'in search of Welshness'. They are in Wales amongst Welshmen. They have no need to fight for their identity, to prove to the Englishman next door that they are different. In contrast, perhaps the exile enjoys announcing that he or she is different, putting on a performance for their English audience (even if the audience isn't that bothered one way or the other)?

Certainly the level of interest shown towards my book *In Search of Welshness* was much greater in the numerous Welsh societies of south-east England than in Llanelli's pubs, or when visiting an Amman Valley pub after Côr Meibion Dyffryn Aman's weekly choir practice, even if many of those present in the pubs personally knew individuals featured in the book. The Carmarthenshire drinkers were typically suspicious. I could see their minds contemplating: 'Who the hell does he think he is?' In contrast, the Welsh exiles in their societies, with their greater sense of *hiraeth*, couldn't wait to get their hands on the book.

Whilst travel writer Jan Morris once offered the opinion that 'by and large the London Welsh are as devoted to Wales as anyone, except that, in the wisdom of their worldliness, they prefer to live well away from the place', the Welsh exile still clings to his or her roots, and some have taken the ultimate decision to return to live in Wales.

This book sets out to explore the attitudes and motivations of a small sample of these returning exiles. They are not a statistically representative sample, but a group of Welsh exiles, many of similar age and education to myself, who have returned to the roots to which I seem so determined to cling. Should this also be me, or does the grass always appear greener on the other side?

Most exiles were initially driven to live in England in search of a livelihood, and after settling are driven to stay, to be near the family and friends that they have acquired over the years.

Such economic requirements and family commitments are also reasons for returning to Wales.

Family responsibilities have forced some to move back, perhaps to look after a sick relative or to be close to siblings. In some of these cases there might still be a preference for their London lifestyle where friends and younger family remain, never forgetting that this London lifestyle might still incorporate a strong Welsh element. It certainly does in my case.

Some have returned to Wales for the same economic reasons they originally left. Whereas once the Welsh came to London in droves in search of work, the cost of living has now driven them in the opposite direction.

Economic reasoning is not only relevant to those short of cash. When considering retirement, the Welsh cost of living and housing buys you much more for your buck than that of the south-east of England.

And many of those interviewed, including those with little in the way of nationalistic leanings, speak of 'the good life' to be had in the hills and along the coastline of Wales. We shouldn't sell the scenic beauty of our homeland short, and meekly acknowledge English taunts about rain and sheep.

The English wives of these exiles speak also of the greater nostalgia their Welsh husbands seem to feel for their childhood. Actor Matthew Rhys, on being interviewed by *The Times*, observed that 'the Welsh do nostalgia very well. If melancholy were an Olympic sport, we'd be gold medallists.'

One solution pursued by some is to have a home in both camps, and such exiles make for interesting interview subjects, able to make a more direct comparison of the two ways of life, if a difference does exist.

And then I have encountered returning exiles with a deeper *hiraeth* for a Welsh-speaking, more socialist, way of life.

And even amongst the many non-Welsh speaking Welshmen there seems to be a yearning for the friendly community spirit that they feel more prominently exists in Wales.

And finally there are the younger working Welsh, some driven back home by the cost of living in south-east England, others wanting to be a part of what they see as a friendlier community, and some who more consciously also want to contribute on a day-to-day basis,working in occupations that help preserve the very economic, political and cultural identity of Wales. This is particularly true of those wanting to use the Welsh language in their daily lives. These may have been happy to sample working life in England, but did so with the clear understanding that it was to be for a limited period only. Wales is home (*cartref*).

Even for those who had spent most of their working life in England, it seemed inevitable for many that they would return to Wales. They had always assumed they would go home some day.

'The draw was, I'm Welsh and I wanted to be in Wales.'

They do recognise that such localism and affinity with the area in which they were raised probably exists in many industrial or rural areas all over the UK, and that it is mainly London and the South East that is seen as austere and unfriendly. The UK is seen as far too focused on London to the detriment of all other regions/countries. They are also aware that Wales has its own problems with its industry and government, or lack of industry and government. Most believe that to solve these problems we need a federal UK incorporating our own assembly to provide a direct influence on Welsh affairs. But no one rates, to put it mildly, the performance of the current assembly incumbents, and few would want complete independence.

Nationhood is not necessarily something that bothers the population of Wales. Yet there is still something that is unique and special about the land of Wales. To quote one returning exile: 'Wales – the best country in the world.'

The final class of exiles I have identified are those who are happy in the bright lights of London, but who still feel sufficient love for their birthplace that they want to make a contribution from a distance to Welsh events and organisations, activities which they hope will generate excitement and pride amongst the resident population, 'their people'.

This is perhaps a more exotic and motivating way of revisiting Wales than just living there, and it recognises that to create and develop its identity, Wales must, just as with the growth of Welsh self consciousness in the late-eighteenth and early-nineteenth century, also look for inspiration and support from exiles living outside its borders.

But how have those who have stayed in Wales reacted to these Welsh exiles and returning Welsh exiles? Is there any sense of resentment from those, particularly Welsh speakers, who feel they have stayed to fight the cause of Welsh media, language and politics whilst others have firstly become part of a brain drain to England, and secondly have returned property rich to buy the homes (sometimes even more than one) that some locals can't afford?

I didn't encounter any consciousness among my returning exiles of such resentment, but perhaps it remains unsaid, and the people to speak to are the inhabitants of Wales themselves.

In addition, Wales continues to experience immigration of a different sort, both from England and the rest of the UK, and from Poland and Eastern Europe.

British immigrants are of three kinds. An inhabitant of a Pembrokeshire coastal village spoke to me of English neighbours whom he didn't know, because they were never there. Their houses were part second homes, part holiday lets for family and friends.

In the Vale of Glamorgan I have also encountered English, Scottish and Irish families who have moved to Wales for work reasons, who have even sent their children to Welsh medium schools in an attempt to integrate into the community, showing a far greater respect and regard for the Welsh language than many of the non-Welsh speaking population who live in this part of south-east Wales.

The final group of English immigrants are retired couples who have come in search of 'the good life' that Wales has to offer, whilst often failing to recognise that they have actually moved to a different country/part of the country with its own particular needs, which are not necessarily being recognised or met by the powers that be in Westminster.

In the last twenty years Wales, like the rest of the UK, has also experienced immigration from Europe, particularly in Carmarthenshire. Local commentators, unlike the sensation-driven tabloids, claim that assimilation, not without its problems, has been relatively pain-free. But perhaps again the people to speak to are the locals and the immigrants themselves.

So both the inhabitants of Wales themselves, and immigrants of non-Welsh heritage, are also worthy of investigation in this search for the meaning of Welshness. But for the moment let us focus on our returning Welsh exiles, and leave these other groups to another time – perhaps another book?

Welsh Excursions

THE WRITING OF this book has provided me with an excuse to visit Wales more often, to interview these returning exiles and see their lifestyle and today's Wales at first hand. My research was then further augmented by continuing some conversations and interviewing additional respondents on the telephone.

My first Welsh visit was to my home town of Llanelli, although en route I took the opportunity to call in on the 2012 National Eisteddfod being held in the Vale of Glamorgan, for me a first visit since the 2000 millennium Eisteddfod in Llanelli. With plans to meet friends on the Eisteddfod field, *y maes*, I booked into the Holiday Inn Express alongside Cardiff Airport, from where I took a shuttle bus to Rhoose railway station to board a train for Llantwit Major, the closest town to the Eisteddfod site.

Not knowing the route taken by the shuttle bus, I enquired of a married couple, my only fellow travellers, the destination of the bus I should seek out for the return trip. The woman replied, with no hint of irony or humour, 'It's quite easy. There's only one bus: it goes from by here to by there, and back again'. A myth had become reality. We really do say such things.

Wales's International Airport at Rhoose obviously does big business. The train, and shuttle service to and from the train, both ran only once each hour throughout the day. And the heavily subsidised train line through the Vale of Glamorgan from Cardiff to Bridgend has unmanned stations and an on-board conductor to take the fares. Even for a major event such as the National Eisteddfod, no extra trains were provided, although another shuttle bus was on hand at Llantwit station to escort the large numbers to the Eisteddfod field.

In true Welsh tradition, the bus echoed with incessant conversation (it sounded as if the whole bus had actually burst into song), and on both days of my visit I ended up sitting alongside someone I knew.

On the first day I encountered a young Japanese Welsh learner (!) whom I had met at a summer school in Aberystwyth two years previously. Her story had in fact provided a fitting conclusion to *In Search of Welshness*. Akiko had been encouraged back in Japan by her English teacher, who hailed from Wales, to come to Cardiff to continue her English studies. She had made many friends in Cardiff, which had persuaded her, with future holidays in mind, to become a Welsh learner. When landing at Heathrow on her last visit, a customs officer had enquired how long she planned to stay, not in Britain but in England. She had replied 'Just for today. I'm merely passing through on my way to Wales.' My book had concluded, 'The world is becoming aware of Wales even if the English are not.'

On my second day's bus journey I sat next to Gareth, a fellow member of the London Welsh Centre in Kings Cross. I remarked how Welsh the atmosphere felt with the intense conversation level being generated by the passengers. He replied by recounting the 'true' story of two German prisoners of war who had escaped during World War Two from the nearby St Asaph camp (apparently the prisoner of war camp had actually been located in nearby Bridgend), disguising themselves as miners in an attempt to make their escape aboard the local colliery bus. The driver immediately drove the bus to the local police station where the prisoners were apprehended. 'I knew they weren't Welsh,' he said. 'They hardly said a word to each other.'

The Eisteddfod was great fun but hard work, as Welsh is the spoken language of the day, and I was in the company of my Welsh tutor and various keen younger Welsh learners whose competence far exceeded mine, despite their having studied the language for significantly less time.

The *maes* was its usual sea of mud, but this didn't seem to deter the presence of 15,000 visitors each day, of all ages, mostly conversing in Welsh.

I managed to sneak into the main pavilion, in those days bedecked all in pink, to witness some of the day's choral competitions. Despite limited exposure, I have grown to like *cerdd dant* or *penillion* singing, which is the art of vocal improvisation to a given melody, the soloist or choir singing a counter melody to a tune played on a harp.

It was quite reassuring to see such a traditional and ancient form of Welsh singing being performed with gusto by young schoolgirl choirs, even if they did resemble St Trinian's in their short skirts and undone neckties. Such an incongruous combination should be witnessed by all who query the value of the Welsh language and culture in today's commercially-oriented world with its cult of celebrity, youth and the globalisation of all things.

The most vivid memory of the Eisteddfod visit was watching a young boy, not quite a teenager, performing a solo break dance in the pouring rain in front of a rock band playing on the large outdoor concert stage, as onlookers cheered from their much drier vantage points under the canopies of the various food and drink stalls. This action summarised the whole atmosphere and ethos of the Eisteddfod for me. An ancient tradition but still capable of being young, trendy and fun. It's unfortunately loss-making, but still worth preserving.

At the Eisteddfod I met Gillian, ex-fellow Welsh learner at the London Welsh Centre in Gray's Inn Road. Gillian has returned to the family home in Newport for economic reasons, in search of a job and a lower cost of living than offered by London. As suggested earlier, whilst the Welsh once came to London in their droves in search of work, the cost of living now drives us back in the opposite direction.

It will be interesting to see whether Gillian has been able to replicate the strong Welsh camaraderie that exists at the London Welsh Centre whilst living in Wales itself, and whether she has continued to find value in Welsh lessons living in non-Welsh speaking Monmouthshire.

Two other London Welsh personnel, former CEO Rhian

Jones and former culture manager Iain Richards, also feature in this book.

Rhian, whilst experimenting with working in England, and earlier France, for intentionally limited periods, categorically sees Wales as home, and most of her career development has involved using Welsh, her first language. She is currently working for Coleg Cymraeg Cenedlaethol, developing and encouraging learning through the medium of the Welsh language. Even her previous work in England and France had a Welsh slant.

Iain, on the other hand, has stayed in London subsequent to his time at the London Welsh Centre. Coming from the mining community of Blackwood he is first and foremost a socialist, and a Valleys boy more than a Welshman. And whilst Valleys life bored him, they are still 'his people' and he has over the last few years created Velvet Coalmine, a rock and literature festival, to bring excitement and pride back to his beloved Blackwood, and he believes he is better able to develop and fund his concept from outside Wales as a precursor to generating local interest. The 2017 festival extends over ten whole days.

These two stories represent the contrasting perspectives and ambitions of the Welsh and non-Welsh speaker, although in their daily working lives both have contributed to preserving Welsh values and identity.

To continue with my visit to Wales, I next journeyed westward from the Eisteddfod to stay with friends Joy and Graham in the village of Hendy, five miles outside Llanelli. Graham had been a major influence in persuading and encouraging me to publish *In Search of Welshness*, and true to form he was also able to furnish me with interesting contacts to incorporate into this second book, focusing as it does on Welsh exiles who have returned to live in Wales.

Graham first introduced me to Huw Jones. Huw has retired to Pontarddulais, the other side of the River Loughor from Hendy, after a career as a teacher and university lecturer, initially in Essex, but mainly in Birmingham and the Midlands.

Huw and his wife Eira, also from Pontarddulais, felt that in retirement there was 'only one place to be', a return 'back home', to be 'comfortable' with people with whom they have a shared identity and values. Theirs was a *hiraeth* for Welsh-speaking Wales and working-class socialism.

Graham and Joy also took me to the seaside resort of Porthcawl, to meet the fascinating ninety-year-old Enid Morris (née Davies), a friend of their aunt. In the 1940s Enid went off to teacher-training college in London, following her father and mother who had just moved there themselves. She herself chose London as a place to study because she claimed she wanted to 'enjoy herself' as well. She eventually moved back to Wales, initially to please her father, and subsequently in support of a new husband whose work was based in Wales. She was happy on her return to Wales but it is clear she must have missed the bright lights of London. Welsh life was 'comfortable', but in the twentieth century many Welsh people also felt the desire to sample a wider, less narrow world. At the same time, much of Enid's London life still focused on the chapels and activities of the London Welsh.

Another exile returning home through necessity is Alan Litherland, whom I visited whilst on holiday in North Wales, at his home in Rhos on Sea, adjacent to Colwyn Bay. Alan hails from the small village of Criccieth on the Llŷn Peninsula, and 'escaped' to join the civil service in London at the tender age of seventeen. He has very fond memories of his schooldays, and is still in regular contact with a handful of his schoolmates, but he had also felt pressurised by the narrowness of Welsh village life.

He settled in North London, and his daughters now live in Watford and Kettering. However, he has spent quite a lot of the intervening years back in Wales, firstly to help his father run the family business, and more recently to be close to his elderly mother. Sadly she passed away in 2015 at the ripe old age of 101. So Alan is now faced with the choice of remaining in Wales or returning to Watford.

So the return from exile can be a question of necessity, the demands of work, finance or family.

Picking up again on my Llanelli excursion, I met up with ex-Llanelli grammarian Geoff Griffiths who has returned to the town after a long career as a senior scientist with the Wellcome Foundation based in Dartford, Kent. Even though a university education and the right employment dictated moving to, and staying in, England, Geoff had always had a hankering from the end of his schooldays for the 'buzz' of London. In his teens he had been a drummer in a rock band, and at the age of eighteen or nineteen all he wanted to do was 'to get out of Llanelli'.

But his Cheshire-born wife feels the Welsh have a far greater depth of nostalgia for their childhood, and in retirement Geoff has sought out his old haunts. He has also come in search of 'the quiet life' across the rolling hills and coast of Carmarthenshire, both more pleasant and cheaper than the bustling south east of England.

He and his wife live in a large, many-bedroomed, detached house above local beauty spot, Swiss Valley, with lovely views of the Gower across the Loughor estuary. Such a house and location couldn't be afforded in Kent.

They are enjoying the much slower pace of life. Jon Gower, in his book *Real Llanelli*, quotes a remark overheard in Llanelli market: "I'll see you later on in a minute now." He concludes 'There's Greenwich Mean. Pacific. Eastern Time. And Llanelli time. Beyond even Einstein's grasp.'

Just down the hill from Geoff's house is the village of Felinfoel, home of rugby icon Phil Bennett and Olympic athlete Dai Green. Also the site of Felinfoel Brewery, the first place in Europe to produce beer in cans - unsurprising given Llanelli's past focus on steel and tinplate.

Geoff used to work for the brewery during his summer vacations from college, so after meeting at his house we wandered down to the village to visit the brewery and a couple of local pubs. We purchased some souvenir glasses emblazoned with the Double Dragon emblem of Felinfoel Ales, and then had a drink in The Greyhound Inn alongside the brewery. Five weeks earlier Charles, Prince of Wales, had trodden the same path and drunk in the very same pub.

Beer was dispensed at the front counter from a series of very synthetic, cosmetic looking fonts, which I assumed served just lagers and keg beers. In preference I requested a 'proper' pint from the wooden, old-fashioned hand pumps that adorned the back counter. The landlord stated that the beer was actually the same. The wooden pumps had only recently been installed just for the benefit of Prince Charles. I have always in fact been suspicious that many Welsh pubs disguise their keg beer as real ale, the coldness and gassiness often giving the game away.

On visiting the loo, I discovered that the Greyhound also acted as a sort of turnstile for Felinfoel RFC whose ground is situated immediately to the rear of the pub.

Just a couple of miles down the road from Felinfoel and Swiss Valley is the centre of Llanelli itself. Always, even in my youth, a fairly robust town, what Jon Gower describes as 'a tribal town', it has acquired a reputation in recent years for a troublesome drug culture. According to one of my returning exiles, Llanelli resident Peter Williams, the media as always overstates the drug problem in the town. He claims it is no different to any other part of the country. Yet he wouldn't walk down Station Road on a Saturday night.

But Peter has a permanent love affair with Llanelli, proof that a sense of *hiraeth* is not solely dependent on being Welsh-speaking. He is a patron of his beloved Scarlets, and was totally convinced he would return to the town, although it has come to pass much later than anticipated, after twenty-nine years in Ascot.

As well as returning exiles, Llanelli has also, since the millennium, experienced a high level of Polish immigration.

Llanelli has encouraged such immigration to a certain extent. According to Jon Gower in his book *Real Llanelli*, in May 2004, 'an employment agency emptied one town in central Poland and brought them all over to Llanelli. They recruited in the Polish town and had an office there. After six months the first wave of migrants brought their children and then the rest of their families over. Once the children entered our education system they proved very adaptable.

'Having a credit union already set up was a godsend. The Saveasy credit union (which shares its office space with the Polish-Welsh Mutual Association) lent £8.5 million over a period of ten years... the sort of (small) loans that the banks wouldn't be disposed to give.'

Chief executive Jeff Hopkins, the former political agent for ex-MP Denzil Davies, says that 'SaveEasy builds on the long tradition of co-operatives in the area, when villages, Trimsaran for example, all had their own co-operatives.'

Peter Williams, mentioned above, is actually the credit union's treasurer. He is aware that the local people and the immigrants have to work harder to get along. The locals must accept that the Poles are not depriving them of employment but undertaking jobs that the indigenous population are not prepared to countenance. And some immigrant families must look outwards more, and work harder at engaging with the local community.

Halina Ashley, the project manager for the Polish-Welsh Mutual Association, and Llanelli resident for the past twenty-one years, claims that Llanelli people have been 'generally welcoming, they find Polish people are good neighbours and respect the fact that the Poles work hard, are conscientious workers. There are those people, of course – many of whom don't work themselves – who begrudge the Poles getting these jobs.'

The other major change to the Llanelli environment since my youth has been the decimation of the town centre by the planners and developers, a story familiar to many towns in the UK.

The problems started as long ago as 1968. Since 1866 Llanelli had possessed an indoor market with a high-ceilinged pavilion so admired across the land as to be accorded the title of Llanelli's 'Crystal Palace'. In 1968 this was replaced by a pokey, low-ceilinged affair buried beneath a multi-storey car park.

Then Tesco, having built a town-centre hypermarket,

moved out of town to the Trostre Retail Park, with a rider to the contract stating that no other food store was permitted on their original town-centre site.

Eventually in 1997, supported by a great fanfare, the St Elli Shopping Precinct was opened in the town centre, although it really only comprised an Asda supermarket supported by a small number of fairly low-key shops. The precinct did, however, provide the locals with a focal avenue for gossip, as they walked through it from Asda to the adjacent indoor market.

Then suddenly, in the millennium, the out-of-town Trostre Retail Park expanded to incorporate two department stores and practically every clothes retailer known to mankind. Also the retailers who represented the mainstay of the town centre itself – Marks and Spencer, Boots, W H Smith – all relocated the mile or so to this new retail focus. And a further Pemberton Retail Park of DIY stores was built alongside, also incorporating the new Parc y Scarlets rugby stadium. The town centre in consequence has become a ghost town of charity shops and seedy pubs.

On my latest visit to Llanelli I decided to explore the atmosphere of the expanded town. The retail park, whilst being an easy and comfortable shopping experience, could have been in any town in the country. This was exacerbated by major retailers such as W H Smith and HMV (now deceased) completely ignoring the values of their Welsh location in the books and music they chose to stock. W H Smith had not one single Welsh-language book on its shelves. Here was a perfect case of anglicisation and globalisation completely obliterating any Welsh or local content.

In contrast, the St Elli precinct, linking Asda and the market, had far more local retailing, and a much more hyperactive atmosphere, in fact a hive of gossip, often in Welsh, very typical of Llanelli market days of old.

In *Real Llanelli*, Jon Gower talks to Barrie Davies, a market enthusiast who runs both a shop in the precinct and a stall in the market itself. 'For him it's "not been a big surprise" that

Asda hasn't brought about the demise of the small businesses which run alongside the supermarket picking up the crumbs off the table, if you like, while Asda gets the main meal. Take curtain track. Customers will worry about saving money on lengths of this but the big stores don't stock the additional gliders you need. We stock the spares the big stores like Asda and B&Q don't.'

But the old main shopping street, Stepney Street, was deserted, except for occasional groups of austere-looking Polish immigrants, at least more austere than I've come to expect from not dissimilar immigration in my local village of Radlett in Hertfordshire.

Off Stepney Street, in the old arcade, was the only Welsh bookshop in the town, and the only retailer outside of W H Smith to stock my first book. I have since learnt that this shop has sadly disappeared. It was never a shopping destination, only an add-on curiosity visit for those shopping in near-by Marks and Spencer. Trade evaporated with the departure of M&S to the new retail park.

Ironically the shop was owned by an Englishman who migrated to Llanelli from Newcastle in the mid-1970s to be with his then girlfriend. He is now a fluent Welsh speaker and nationalist. I enquired about my book. As the first of any such enquiry he immediately identified me as the author, and asked me to sign his only, and unsold copy, to see if this might help generate a sale. I also bought a book of Welsh poetry, thus losing out in the economic equation, generating more sales for the shop than it had achieved on my behalf.

All is not lost in Llanelli however. There are no plans for Stepney Street, but a new development, Eastgate, occupying the eastern section of the old town centre, has just been created, with cinemas, a theatre, and several pubs, cafes and restaurants. Although it would have been nicer if it had incorporated a retail presence, and a non-mass market one at that. But there is still hope. *Yma o hyd*.

On this latest visit I also took the risk of sampling Llanelli's nightlife in the company of old school friend Hugh (not Huw) Edwards. We met in Wetherspoons, housed in the old Llanelly Cinema. I was led to expect a den of iniquity, but the brewers had preserved the elegance of the old cinema, and the clientele was nicely mixed, of all ages and persuasions, certainly more salubrious in my experience than the Wetherspoons in Borehamwood, Hertfordshire, next to the so-called Elstree television studios.

Hugh and I also enjoyed a curry next door in the Sheesh Mahal. I had one of the tastiest curry dishes I have ever sampled. The restaurant was in fact named Welsh Curry House of the Year in both 2008 and 2011. It was just sad that both pub and restaurant are part of a block of buildings in the western part of Stepney Street which looked ripe for demolition.

Llanelli is not short of haute cuisine. With Joy and Graham I sampled other culinary delights the town has to offer, including lunch at the Machynys Peninsula Golf Club, and dinner at Sosban, a stunningly renovated, grade II listed, ex-Victorian pump house, resembling a church from its exterior, adjacent to the old North Dock. The latter, the AA's Welsh Restaurant of the year 2012–13, is jointly owned by Simon Wright, restaurateur and food broadcaster, ex-Wales rugby internationals, Stephen Jones and Dwayne Peel, and construction entrepreneur Robert Williams.

So Llanelli is not devoid of style. It has just lost a lot of its character. The harshness was always there.

But today's Cardiff, a mere forty-five minute drive away, no further than our frequent excursions to the centre of London, offers far more culture, both popular and highbrow, than in the 1950s of my youth.

And my fellow exiles, after their working-class upbringings, are returning with middle-class mores. It is just to be hoped that they give a Welsh not English slant to these mores, in terms of accent, culture and personality. Byron Rogers recalls that 'what passed for a middle class in Carmarthen spoke with the most exaggerated English accents.' In contrast today, prize-winning restaurant Sosban has a Welsh-spelt name and an ethos which is identified as 'no pomp or fuss: drink, eat and be merry'. Perhaps some things have changed for the better, and we can appreciate culture without giving it an arrogant English slant.

A worst-case scenario is that the pleasant lifestyle of rural living becomes divorced and separated from adjacent harsher urban environments. This, after all, is what has happened in the Thames Valley along the M4 corridor.

Several of my old friends have returned to Wales to more attractive rural idylls. Their motivations also incorporate in some instances the desire to preserve Welsh values and to contribute to a stronger Welsh economy.

Cledwyn Davies, a Post Office executive and London client of mine, couldn't resist the opportunity to return to Wales as the marketing manager for Wales and the Marches Postal Board. He and his wife subsequently acquired a sub-post office in Llangain in rural Carmarthenshire, before retiring with his family to an idyllic spot in Nantgaredig in the Towy Valley above Carmarthen. Cledwyn's last post before retirement was as marketing and innovation manager of Coleg Sir Gâr, working with local industries to develop skills through training. He has clearly done his bit to contribute to Welsh industry and commerce, and his English-born wife, Suzanne, is doing her utmost to preserve Wales's musical traditions, singing in a choir and playing in both a brass and a wind orchestra.

En route back to London, after my visit to Llanelli, I called in on my old college friend, Roger Banner, who lives in splendid isolation two miles off the Monmouth to Abergavenny road in rural Gwent. The house is approached down a single-track lane with frequent 100-yard stretches devoid of any passing places, where it is impossible to even open the car doors because of the encroaching hedgerows. I spent a sleepless night at the house dreaming of massive farm vehicles forcing me to reverse in a straight line back over hundreds of yards. Come the morning we also discovered that the lane was about to receive a new surface of tar, and I only departed from the house in the nick of time before the invasion of the road maintenance traffic. Even then I was forced to turn inland and negotiate a further five miles of such tracks before returning to the sanity of a two-carriageway main road.

Roger, originally from Newport, retired to this rural paradise, initially to be near his sons, whose education he had decided to place in the capable hands of Monmouth School. But he claims that subconsciously he 'always assumed he would come back to Wales.' The decision has been totally vindicated, with Roger and his wife finding the level of neighbourliness and friendship far outweighing anything experienced previously in Teddington and Wentworth in England's Home Counties. Roger has also kept himself active, taking on the role of accountant for our alma mater, Aberystwyth University.

Another returning exile, Richard Davies, I first met decades ago at the Cambrian Lawn Tennis Club, hidden away in the North-London suburb of Cricklewood. His brother, Lod, before his recent untimely demise, was still a prominent and active member of the London Welsh Centre in Gray's Inn Road.

They come from a London Welsh family but both were evacuated to the vicinity of Aberystwyth during the Second World War, and Richard was in fact born in the town. Richard also married a Welsh girl who hails from Penybont in Powys, and after retirement they have moved back to the area to live alongside a sixteen-acre smallholding. Richard sees himself as very clearly Welsh, and always had an overwhelming desire to live in Wales, with a particular ambition to have a go at farming. Raised on a farm near Aberystwyth, he is also a Welsh speaker, but Ceredigion is too Welsh-speaking for his non-Welsh speaking wife, so they have settled instead in her home county of Powys.

Both Richard and his wife are very active in the locality, and theirs is a very interesting story in which they find themselves experiencing the mix of Welsh community values with the views of local retired English couples who fail to see Wales as a different country needing special attention from Westminster, a community which is also trying to accommodate the presence of younger immigrants from eastern Europe who in their search for work are also having to adapt to a new life in a strange country.

The other tactic of Welsh exiles in search of their roots is to become a two-home family. Two such exiles are ex-Llanelli grammarians Peter Lane and Tony Jenkins. Over a period of six months both generously invited me to stay in their West Wales homes so I could attend two separate Llanelli Grammar School Old Boys' reunions. It is typically Welsh that there should be two such old pupil associations running in parallel, or even in competition, with each other.

The first dinner I attended was held in the old school buildings themselves, and was organised to formally dedicate a wall plaque in honour of those old boys who had perished in the two world wars. It was also planned as a celebration of the centenary of the opening of the school, only for the organisers to belatedly discover that they were a few decades out. (It is rumoured that Llanelli RFC also got their timing wrong, although not to such an extreme extent, when celebrating the club's centenary in 1972).

This commemorative dinner was organised despite the presence of the Old Boys' Association annual dinner held in January every year at the Stradey Park Hotel. The grammar school actually ceased to exist in 1976, becoming Y Graig Comprehensive, one of six such schools across Llanelli, and the old boys' association is meant to incorporate past pupils of both the grammar school and the later comprehensive.

Llanelli, until some recent advances by Plaid Cymru, has always been part of the socialist heartland, and very much a supporter of the possibly more democratic comprehensive-school concept. But one has to admit that the introduction of such schools in general across the country has been very badly handled – introduced in some areas and not others, often co-existing alongside grammar schools which would cream off the better pupils and staff. And the ethos of the schools themselves has, to me, seemed to be focused on providing a syllabus for the lowest common denominator, as opposed to a streaming of abilities. By all means aspire to democracy, but not to the discouragement of ability. God forbid if this makes me a Tory. I think not. Conservatism is much more about the protection of those with wealth as opposed to ability.

The comprehensive system certainly does not seem to have generated the pupil pride which we old boys felt and feel for Llanelli Boys' Grammar School.

I approached these old boys' dinners with a certain amount of trepidation, anticipating a forum for individuals to bring to everyone's attention how well they had succeeded in the wider world since leaving school. In contrast, both evenings were full of camaraderie and nostalgia, with an overriding impression of pride in the school, and a gratefulness for success achieved as a result of the education received from the very-well-thought-of academic staff. Unfortunately, many of the diners, not dissimilar to pupils of Byron Rogers's Queen Elizabeth School, Carmarthen, no longer lived in Llanelli, nor possibly, Wales.

Llanelli's academic record, I believe, did dip with the introduction of comprehensive schools. Certainly in sporting prowess, with intra-town competition between the town's six comprehensive schools replacing the far more competitive inter-town rivalry between the various grammar schools spread across the breadth of South Wales. The baton to develop young rugby talent has instead been passed to the academies established by the four major Welsh rugby clubs/regions.

The situation seems to be improving, however. One of Llanelli's comprehensives is the well-respected Welsh language school, Ysgol y Strade, and the old grammar school building in which we sat down to dine has become a flourishing sixth-form college, Coleg Sir Gâr, with 12,000 students and strong links with the University of Wales Trinity St David's, a merger of the University of Wales, Lampeter and Trinity College, Carmarthen. The meal itself was excellently provided by the school's catering students based at Pibwrlwyd, the agricultural studies campus just outside Carmarthen.

On the sporting front, in 2012 Sir Gâr won the Rosslyn Park Public School Rugby Sevens (evidence unfortunately of our acknowledgement of the pre-eminence of English-run sporting competitions). It was, however, the first time a town school had achieved the honour since the Grammar School won the competition four times in six years in the late 1950s/early 1960s, before being withdrawn by headmaster Stanley Rees after accusations of professionalism. Before the recent success of Coleg Sir Gâr, the only other achievement by a Llanelli school had been that of the Welsh-medium school, Ysgol y Strade, who also reached the final on one occasion.

For the first dinner, to commemorate old boys who had perished in the Second World War, my old school friend and fellow London marketing man, Peter Lane, kindly asked me, along with fellow old boys, orthopaedic surgeon Tudor Thomas and keynote speaker Lord Griffiths of Burry Port, to stay at his large Victorian house in Oystermouth alongside Mumbles, overlooking the wide attractive curve that is Swansea Bay.

Peter and his wife Margaret had previously lived in Chingford in Essex, and on the death of her father, they decided to once again buy an apartment in Chingford, whilst still maintaining their house in South Wales.

Peter, unlike his namesake Peter Williams, does not have a love affair with Llanelli. He lives the 'good life' in the middle class Swansea suburb of Oystermouth, with its scenery and pleasant environment, and its accessibility to the culture that Swansea, and Cardiff in particular, have to offer. He finds attending the opera at Cardiff Bay's Millennium Centre a much less daunting prospect than travelling into the centre of London from Chingford. The world of Llanelli, on the other hand, he feels he would find slightly too inward-looking. He is nevertheless a Scarlets debenture holder.

On the day following the dinner, all roads led to Parc y Scarlets, where the Scarlets were entertaining the then

European Champions, Leinster, in their first home game of the 2012–13 Heineken Cup campaign. After a drink in the Phil Bennett Suite we sat resplendent in Peter's prime debenture seats at the top of the South Stand.

Unfortunately the game wasn't a sell-out, and sad to say, I found the ground atmosphere distinctly muted when compared with the noise generated by the organised chants of visiting supporters in the English Aviva Premiership, which I experienced at the Kassam Stadium in Oxford, London Welsh's home when they gained promotion to England rugby's top table for the first time. The chants of these English clubs are, however, very manufactured and forced, and I still fondly recall the dynamic pervading influence of the spontaneous singing of the Scarlets' visiting throngs at London Irish in the 2009 Heineken Cup, and at Harlequins in the 2013–14 competition.

But the Welsh public in general haven't taken to the regionalisation of Welsh rugby. The regions were an artificial creation imposed on an already-existing framework of clubs with strong historic support. It was asking a lot of Pontypridd fans, for example, to support Cardiff Blues.

Commercially and financially Wales may struggle to justify more than four teams, but having such a small number of teams also creates its own problems. As well as not appealing to the above-mentioned historical support, four teams reduces the number of competitive derby matches, makes a Welsh Cup meaningless, and provides too small a stage for enough potential stars of the future to exhibit their skills, especially with the additional influx of overseas players. The Scarlets did not have a home match between 8 December 2012 and 19 January 2013. In my childhood, Llanelli RFC had four home games in Christmas week alone.

Also, with only four regions, practically every game is televised, providing the easy option for potential supporters to stay at home and watch the games on TV. This is even more likely, given the strange kick-off times of Friday and Sunday evenings adopted by the Pro 12 League, who seem to have given satellite broadcasters and the English leagues first claim to the prime weekend time slots. The Scarlets region, being geographically quite large, is further hampered by the distances supporters have to travel to attend matches at such inappropriate times.

I have a suspicion that introducing additional clubs/regions would increase rather than decrease earning potential, although it would obviously reduce the proportion of central funding received by each individual region. The WRU in any case ought to be carrying more of the financial burden, especially when it comes to the wages of Welsh squad members who are often not available to play for their regions. A review of the chaotic fixture list would also not go amiss.

With struggling Welsh regions, it remains a mystery how our national side continues to rise to the occasion in the Six Nations every few years, even if continuity of success proves elusive, and we still seem incapable of matching the might of the southern hemisphere.

A successful Welsh rugby team is of such crucial importance, given that support for the national side is one of very few outward signs that allow Welsh men and women to parade their nationality.

To return to the subject of old boys' reunions, my presence at the year's second dinner, the annual January get together, was encouraged by ex-grammarian Tony Jenkins, resident of both Twickenham and the little seaside village of Pwll, just west of Llanelli. Tony has become my de facto South Wales sales manager for *In Search of Welshness*, given that he is continually recommending it to his friends, and he encouraged my presence at the dinner partly to sign a few copies.

Also present at the dinner was Scarlets' chaplain, Eldon Phillips, well known for officiating at Ray Gravell's funeral, and at the thanksgiving service held to honour Stradey Park prior to its demolition, and those supporters whose ashes had been scattered over the pitch across the years.

The Rev Eldon is a curry lover, and as a regular customer

of the Ali Raj Brasserie in Llanelli's Trinity Road, he has been accorded the honour of having a dish named after him. Eldon agreed to buy a copy of *In Search of Welshness* if I agreed to sample his curry.

Tony Jenkins has to some extent purchased a second home in Wales partly to reconnect with the friendships and community of his youth. Also in attendance at the dinner was Geoff Griffiths from Swiss Valley. Both he and Tony Jenkins had been Carmarthenshire county tennis champions in years gone by; they in fact spent most of the evening debating which of them had won the title most often.

Whilst we were at the dinner, Llanelli and South Wales were hit by one of the worst storms in living memory, and our taxi had to return to Tony's house in Pwll via the mountain road through Stradey Woods, as the coastal road was flooded.

Another friend and ex Llanelli tennis champion, Jeff Harry, failed to make the dinner at all, as his fifty-mile journey from Tenby had taken him all of three hours, with the water at times up to his car's wheel arches.

The following morning was, however, all calmness and serenity, and we were able to breakfast in Tony's upstairs sitting room and admire the fine views of the whole of the Gower Peninsula, including watching several 4x4 vehicles out cockle picking at low tide. Apparently when pursuing this second home, it had been a straight choice for Tony and his wife between Pwll and Provence. Pwll won.

The Saturday after the dinner once again involved watching rugby, this time as spectators at Llanelli RFC's cup match against Pontypridd. It is sad that, with Scarlets regional matches possessing much greater significance, few supporters also take the time to follow the exploits of the RFC club's semi-professional side in the Welsh Premiership.

On this occasion, Llanelli spectators were far outnumbered by the very vocal and loyal visiting Pontypridd support, a fan base which the regional set-up has failed to entice away to watch Cardiff Blues. The contrasting level of support for the two teams clearly illustrates the two sides of the same failed WRU-inspired coin.

The Saturday evening saw me once again sampling the delights of Sosban, Stephen Jones's restaurant in Llanelli's North Dock, and I was also treated, along with Tony and his wife Catriona, to an excellent Sunday lunch at the home of Geoff and Julia Griffiths.

In my travels researching this second book I have encountered much wonderful Welsh hospitality, only serving to enhance my biased opinion of us as a warm and welcoming nation.

Wales Revisited

So MUCH FOR my own short-term experiences. What else can these exiles expect on their return to Wales, in some cases, many decades after their original departure?

First of all, are the Welsh actually friendlier, or is it a myth?

Reporter Selma Chalabi, of English, Scottish and Arabic blood, but having lived in Wales for most of her adult life, undertook a project for BBC Radio Wales's *Eye on Wales*, investigating what it meant to be Welsh in this twenty-first century, specifically focusing on one community, Senghenydd, at the far end of the Aber Valley in Caerphilly county.

She asked people to give her words that for them encapsulated Welshness. Words such as passion, warmth, open-hearted and welcoming repeatedly surfaced. Words, she suggested, that were unlikely to appear in a description of Englishness.

But we are also far from perfect. We have our negative side. Those interviewed by Selma Chalabi perceived the Welsh as hemmed-in, self-doubting, insecure and cynical. For me this is cynical not in the sense of achieving objectives at whatever cost, but a doubting, suspicious sort of cynicism, always mocking the efforts made by others, bred, I suggested earlier, from the perceived need to become English and cease to be Welsh if one wanted to succeed in life.

Whilst recently dining out in Llanelli with fellow diners who had been forewarned about my search for Welshness, I inadvertently used the phrase 'my home village' to describe my current abode in Radlett, Hertfordshire.

'Oh, so that's home to you now is it?' came the retort. So typically Welsh.

Add to this a reticence in taking risks and a love of forming committees every time a decision needs to be taken, and we have ample reasons why the Welsh are finding it difficult to govern themselves.

The English, in contrast, even my many genuine and honest English friends, believe they represent the centre of the universe. And this total sense of entitlement is an attitude which is partly encouraged by a one-eyed, xenophobic press.

In its world, Wales ceases to exist. Englishness is assumed to represent the whole of the UK. The media insists on talking about 'British reserve' and 'the British stiff upper lip' when the gregarious and emotional Welsh have no such qualities.

And it is astonishingly ironic that the UK Government are insisting that immigrants acquire a knowledge and understanding of the 'British' history and way of life, when the English know absolutely nothing at all about Wales or the Celtic fringe of this so-called United Kingdom. They are not even prepared or interested in trying to learn. We are dismissed as an irrelevance.

When not being ignored in the press, Wales is belittled. Byron Rogers, in his book *Three Journeys*, talks of Welsh exiles gossiping in the basement of long-gone Welsh bookseller, Griffs, just off the Charing Cross Road, whilst 'all the time the unseen feet of the master race clattered on the gratings overhead, just as they had clattered on 600 years of Welsh history'.

I write this on the day an article appeared in *The Times*, written by one Valentine Low, announcing that Denmark had purchased the new Welsh drama series *Hinterland* incorporating both Welsh and English dialogue. Mr Low argues that, 'it is sheer coincidence that Denmark, the country that brought the world *The Killing*, has now turned to Wales for a new series about a brooding detective with a past', when they themselves (the Danes, and by assumption, the Welsh) are also 'a gloomy folk from a melancholy land who speak a strange, unpronounceable language, but are usually prepared to switch to English should the occasion demand it.' He couldn't have been more rude, pompous or condescending if he had tried.

I think the Wales of today is probably far more developed

culturally than the Wales of my own childhood. Live entertainment venues now abound, at least in Cardiff, compared to the Wales of 1971, when Sir Geraint Evans, world-renowned tenor, threatened never to sing again in Wales unless facilities for opera were improved.

And much of the new development has a Welsh slant to it. We have national Welsh orchestras, a jazz orchestra, opera, Welsh pop groups that sing in Welsh, a new wave of young mixed-sex Welsh choirs etc, etc. But according to Siôn Jobbins, in an article in *Cambria Magazine* in 2009, something has been lost:

'The Welsh genius is to adapt, translate, and colonise musical forms from the Italian triple harp of the seventeenth century, which we made our own, to sea-shanties, hymns, Handel's Messiah to rap and pop... But I feel something is being lost in the Welsh singing world today.

'Despite today's bravado, Welsh singing is suffering from a lack of self-confidence. The new wave of sweet-smelling, young, mixed-sex choirs give the impression of a healthy tradition, but how many of them are now part of that tradition and could sing a "traditional" Welsh tune? When the last of our sweaty, blazer-wearing male voice choirs fade away in twenty years' time, who will sing our hymns? What will replace them?

'Our Assembly seems too shy or too downright embarrassed to promote or finance Welsh music or arts. The Irish Republic's Arts Council in 2005/6 spent £10.72 per head of population on the arts. Wales spent £8.80. Where money has been spent, priorities have been skewed... Price (former Plaid Cymru MP, Adam Price) noted that our national opera company has never appointed a Welsh musical director or staged a Welsh opera. Adam's argument wasn't against staging foreign operas. His argument is simple: where's the national platform and support for a Welsh Dvořák or Sibelius?

'The National Opera's budget is £6.3 million of the Welsh Arts Council's money. But the budget for the "traditional" Welsh music foundation, Trac, is £274,000. I'm certainly not arguing for cutting

71

the opera company's budget, but rather increasing the money given to forms of music which are played only in Wales...

'At the moment the budget for "Heritage, Sport and the Welsh Language" is a mere £160m – less than 1.5% of the Assembly's budget.'

Our returning exiles via participation or encouragement perhaps need to do something to redress this balance.

But in my youth, things were much worse. The culture offered us non-Welsh speakers by classical music and English-language theatre and literature was divorced from Wales and Welsh culture. It was totally of English origin (the world of Elgar, Shakespeare and Dickens), and the enjoyment of it had a distinct snob appeal, encouraging anglicisation amongst the Welsh middle classes.

Byron Rogers in *Three Journeys* reflects that: 'What passed for a middle class in Carmarthen spoke with the most exaggerated English accents... deliberately mispronouncing place names. They did not speak Welsh in our town, or if they did, they kept quiet about it.'

And on moving away to London: 'there were those who did not see it as exile, and severed all links with their past, being men who were making their way in the professions and, being usually called Jones; accountants and hospital consultants who had hyphens materialise in their surnames like the black monoliths in the film 2001. It was after all, part of the Welsh way of getting on.'

Byron does, however, concede that it was also possible not to have any of this, but 'to live in London in a lunar base of Welsh exile' comprising the Welsh chapels, the London Welsh Rugby Club, and Saturday nights at the London Welsh Centre in Gray's Inn Road. A world with which I am only too familiar.

But what of my fellow exiles with their working-class upbringings now returning to Wales, having been exposed to middle-class English mores?

They will at least find a population where speaking Welsh

has now become a status symbol, even in previously-anglicised Cardiff, with monoglot English-speaking parents attempting to learn Welsh to keep up with their bilingual offspring.

But within this newly-acquired Welsh confidence about identity, there are still two dangers. The battle to develop Welsh as a genuine actively spoken every day and official language still has to be won. The 2011 Census results show a decline in the number of Welsh speakers from 21% to 19% of the population, and although the percentages are higher amongst schoolchildren, Welsh is not the language of the playground or Facebook, and not all children are confident of their ability to speak the language once they have left school.

There is also a reverse threat, the long-standing danger of ostracising non-Welsh speakers.

There is a joke going the rounds in Wales of a man coming across a lifeguard on duty whilst out walking along the sands of Swansea Bay. When a swimmer out at sea gets into trouble and screams for help, the lifeguard doesn't respond.

'Why aren't you going to his rescue?' asks the walker.

'I can't swim,' replies the lifeguard.

'So how did you get the job?' questions the walker.

'Well, I'm a Welsh speaker, aren't I,' comes the reply.

Selma Chalabi in her project on Welsh identity quotes former Plaid Cymru MP Adam Price as arguing that the language issue 'cuts both ways. It creates a deeper sense of national identity and gives us a tangible source of distinctiveness. On the other hand, in some people's eyes, it does divide us between two communities. It's as if being Welsh is some sort of sliding scale. That is a problem for us here in Wales, and one that we haven't fully worked through yet.'

I personally thought it was encouraging that some non-Welsh speakers 'saw themselves as less Welsh precisely because they couldn't speak Welsh; they had this sense they were missing some vital aspect of what it means to be Welsh.'

Prof. Tony Manstead, who was part of the research team, said, 'Among Welsh speakers, their attitude to the Welsh language and how important it is to speak Welsh depended on their perception of the relationship with England. The more unfair they saw the relationship with England, the more important they thought it was to speak Welsh. If they thought the relationship was unfair, but improving, they were less keen to see the Welsh language as being the way to define yourself as Welsh.'

The Wales to which my exiles have returned also differs in other ways from the Wales of their childhoods. It has been affected by influences which are also prevalent in every other part of the UK.

The first of these is the blight of the town planners who have done their utmost to decimate the character and identity of most towns and cities across Britain.

To quote Byron Rogers on his home town of Carmarthen: 'For the town is dying. In the late-twentieth century the council planners pulled down its old alleys, demolished the narrow street which was all that remained of a town gate, and erased the streets that had housed the Carmarthen Mob. An eyesore these might have been, but it was our eyesore; it had a character, an identity, and in its place has come the newly-developed centre of the nowhere town. The district and the county councils have severed its past from Carmarthen.

'For the empires are back, it is just they have other names. Like Debenhams. And Morrisons. And Tesco. Tesco, having already built on the medieval friary, has now moved on to build the biggest, or second biggest, megastore in Wales, this on the outskirts of a town with a population of only 15,000. It is a vast cancer which will suck the life out of the commercial centre of Carmarthen. My town is a trading post now, the cash it generates streaming out of the town.'

And Siôn Jobbins writes in *Cambria* magazine about Swansea's misfortune to be 'blitzed in the 1940s only to be reconstructed with the charm of East European Communism... Swansea's peeling streets seem unloved even by its own people.' All the result of local government in Wales, 'the spiv end of capitalism married to the latest Socialist anti-individual, big state brutalism.'

But there are towns which have avoided this planning 'blitz'. Roger Banner, who has retired to Monmouth, but still stays active as an unpaid member of the governing council of Aberystwyth University, speaks of both these market towns as expanding outwards across the decades without succumbing to the blight of out-of-town retail centres. They have thus still preserved the character of their original high streets with their range of traditional shops. And the exposure of both these towns to more limited levels of immigration than encountered elsewhere also means that they have retained much more of their local identity.

Roger thinks that Aberystwyth has in fact changed little in character since our student days, and may today have an even stronger Welsh presence. He is not certain however that exclusively Welsh-speaking halls of residence at the university are necessarily a move in the right direction, and questions whether they strike the correct balance between preserving the Welsh language and avoiding a schism between Welsh and non-Welsh speakers.

Wales in general has also suffered more than most from the policy of successive UK governments of not supporting home-based primary industry and manufacturing in the face of cheaper overseas alternatives. The Wales of coal and steel is a thing of the past, and there is a great industrial vacuum in its place.

A century ago, Wales, or at least the South Wales coalfield, was one of the world's growth economies (not that the Welsh themselves were the main benefactors).

John Osmond, until recently of the Institute of Welsh Affairs, argues that much of this industrial success came, apart obviously from the natural resources, from what he calls 'connectivity'. You could travel by train (although not high-speed train, I might add) from any town in Wales to any other town. And, more importantly, one could access any other country across the globe via the thriving South Wales ports.

In contrast, the Wales of today is industrially described as having 'a general crisis of underperformance'. We have only one motorway (what John Osmond calls a 'joke' motorway), and just Rhoose for an airport, which the Welsh Government has bought to save its very existence.

Any planned developments, such as rail electrification, involve the west-east route to England. And David Cameron even reneged on paying for this. Wales's industrial existence is totally dependent on feeding off England. There is still no direct road or rail link between North and South Wales.

Although ironically, modern phone and internet communication could actually be capable of producing an industrial structure which is less dependent on the quality of transport available. Do tell the proposers of HS2, as the Welsh taxpayer is still expected to contribute to this new London–North of England transport link.

Whilst there is little or no industry, people's demands continue to grow with the expectations generated by the consumerist society in which we live. No wonder we have teenage suicides in Bridgend and a drug culture in my home town of Llanelli.

Nothing is helped by the demise of the two rocks that kept Welsh society together in past times of industrial stress. I speak of religion and the trade unions.

As described earlier, Wales a century ago was probably one of the most religious countries in the world. Between the mid-eighteenth and mid-nineteenth centuries Wales experienced fifteen major religious revivals, resulting in its reputation as the 'Land of Revivals'. In contrast, Wales is now probably one of the least religious countries on the globe. Nearly a third of those completing the 2011 Census forms claim to have no religion. Only 58% called themselves Christian, a fourteen-point decline since 2001, a larger decrease than to be found in any English region.

The nineteenth and twentieth centuries also saw first the growth then the demise of heavy industry and with it the loss of power and relevance of the trade unions.

In 1913 the coal industry was Wales's largest employer, accounting for over a quarter of the male labour force. South Wales produced 20% of the UK's coal output and 30% of coal exports. Cardiff was the largest coal-exporting port in the world.

All that now remains are a few drift and opencast mines, plus one small deep mine. The last large deep mine, Tower Colliery, having been run as a miners' co-operative since 1994, finally closed in 2008.

The failed Miners' Strike of the 1980s was fought and lost in Wales on a nationalistic as well as an industrial platform, as the removal of the coal mines has proved a body blow to the Welsh economy and the livelihood of its people.

It is ironic that we are bemoaning the loss of coal mining, after the previous generation had worked so hard to pay for the education of their offspring, to save them from also having to experience the harsh and inhuman working environments that were the steelworks and the coal mine.

We should not bemoan the loss of such an existence. The problem lies not with the demise of the coal and steel industries but with the lack of alternative employment, and the absence of anyone to argue our case.

'West Wales' and 'the Valleys' are both designated as amongst Europe's poorest regions, possessing only 68% (down from 76% in 1999) of the wealth of the average European region. They thus qualified for the third time in 2013 for a European grant. This so called Convergence Programme (previously Objective One) requires matched funding on the part of the recipients. In Wales's case this has to come partly from raiding the Assembly's core budgets, as both the recent coalition government and the previous Labour government refused to contribute, not only towards Welsh funding but also funding for struggling English and Scottish regions.

The arrival of Brexit and the removal of the need for a

UK contribution to an overall European budget will help the average British taxpayer, but it is estimated that it will cost Wales £400m in lost grants. It is hoped that Westminster, with pressure from the Welsh Assembly, will make good the shortfall. Don't hold your breath.

Internal UK financial budgets allocated to the Celtic countries are adjusted from historical levels by the Barnett Formula which is based purely on population size. It takes no account of age or fiscal need, unemployment rates or health, nor sparsity of population, nor cost of travel.

The Welsh Assembly has no say in how much money it is given, no power to raise taxes, at least for the moment, and no control over how its own taxes are spent by the UK Government. What use, I ask you, is Crossrail or HS2 to Wales?

Yet the money that is handed over to the Welsh Assembly for such things as health and education is also not guaranteed to be wisely spent. And the Assembly has to date been unsuccessful in producing improvements in the economies of West Wales and the Valleys with the European grants received.

Martin Shipton's book on the first ten years of the new Welsh Assembly is appropriately entitled *Poor Man's Parliament*. In 1999 the incumbent UK Labour Government succeeded in creating a new legislative body with minimum power and authority. One has to ask the question whether they in fact wanted it to succeed at all. The Assembly does not have the power to set its own budgets, and only after a referendum in 2011 did it gain the right to set its own laws and policies. Previously permission had to be sought on an individual case basis from Westminster via an extremely convoluted administrative process.

Not that you'd have been aware of the referendum, as some 'national' daily newspapers couldn't even be bothered to cover the event, and many people refused to vote because they claimed they had insufficient knowledge of the issues involved.

And finally, with more than 600 years of 'colonial' rule,

Wales has had little or no experience in the art of government, and such skills can't be learned overnight.

In the aftermath of the 2015 general election, what strikes one is, firstly, how little the Welsh population are aware of the political happenings, given the minimal coverage Wales receives in the media. Apparently, they are totally unaware of how Wales gained financially from being in Europe. And even thought the major election issue was health, a responsibility which is devolved to the Cardiff Assembly and not relevant to elections for Westminster.

Secondly, whilst Cameron and his cronies, in the lead-up to the 2015 election, played lip-service to increasing the powers of the Welsh Assembly, the offer was extremely vague, and clearly less than the Scots are managing to achieve as a result of their own referendum. And with the onset of Brexit, we are going to require even more support from Westminster to compensate for the loss of European funding.

The final element of change to be found in Wales at the turn of the new century is the increasing level of immigration.

Llanelli has acquired the nickname of 'Llane-ski' because rumour has it that the town's population of 40,000-plus has been bolstered by at least 2,000 (5%) Polish immigrants, with a further 8,000 estimated to be living in the nearby Gwendraeth Valleys.

Carmarthenshire official figures, however, suggest 2,000 is a closer estimate of the number of Poles in the county as a whole, accounting for just under 1% of the total population. These same figures claim that Poles are concentrated in three locations: Carmarthen, Llanelli and, thirdly, Llanybydder, where they make up a massive 12% of the population. In Llanybydder and Llanelli their employment is dominated by a small number of very large employers, but in Carmarthen, Poles are more dispersed amongst smaller operations.

Poles came to Carmarthenshire in two waves. The first, from 2004 to 2006, consisted mostly of single men from small towns in Poland brought over by agencies to work in food-processing operations. Since 2006 their composition has changed, with more families, more direct employment, less agency work, and a wider spread of origins in Poland. Poles are increasingly living in private rented accommodation, bringing their families over, and having children in Wales.

Poles have a popular reputation as heavy drinkers. A report commissioned by Dyfed-Powys Drug Intervention Programme to study substance abuse amongst Poles in Carmarthenshire states that this reputation is deserved, but the evidence to suggest that such drinking is more pronounced than in the local population is mixed. However, the Poles drink differently from the Welsh. They drink at home and in public places and not the pub. Thus a Llanelli councillor has blamed a rise in drinking on the streets on the influx of Polish workers. Yet much Polish crime seems to go unreported as at home there is a strong sense that things 'stay in the family', and the Poles in general try hard to steer clear of the police.

As far as drugs are concerned, the predominantly British service providers had almost no knowledge of Polish drug use. In focus groups, the Poles themselves also suggested that usage was almost non-existent, but individually were much more open. Yet there have been no Poles arrested for drugs. Consumption is mainly at home, and they do not deal in drugs in sufficient quantities to interest the police. Most Polish suppliers are just acting as intermediaries for friends, or buying in bulk for parties, whereas the main known drug-dealers are of British origin.

Jon Gower writes, 'There have been isolated incidents of anti-Polish graffiti appearing on walls and the media have sometimes turned a selective spotlight on the immigration, but generally Llanelli has absorbed the new immigrants as it has nationalities in the past, in the heyday of heavy industry.'

Wales has previously had high levels of immigration, particularly with the development of the South Wales coalfield in the latter part of the nineteenth century and the early part of the twentieth century. Such immigration was both from Europe plus a large number of English immigrants. Many immigrants settled in the valleys of Glamorgan and Gwent, and it is interesting to note that whilst these are not, as a result, high Welsh-speaking areas, they now represent those areas of the country where the highest percentage of the population in the 2011 Census claimed to be 'Welsh'. Wales has obviously succeeded in uniting subsequent generations of these immigrants 'under the dragon'.

The 2011 Census actually puts immigration to Wales at a lower level than other parts of the UK – excluding, that is, the increasing number of English crossing Offa's Dyke to live.

Many of my sample of returning Welsh exiles could be classified into this group of older, city-based home buyers, retiring or downsizing to our so-called Principality.

If not English, many are non-Welsh speakers and the villages in which they have settled are in danger of losing their traditional Welsh character.

Such a village is Brechfa, population 300, north east of Carmarthen in the Cothi Valley, situated on a B-road off the A40. According to Caroline Evans, secretary of Llanihangel Rhos y Corn and Brechfa Community Association, (Wales Online, 22 January 2013): 'Brechfa is taking stock of how it can survive as a village. Last year, the chapel was closed and put up for sale. This year, the falling numbers of children in Ysgol Brechfa has meant that governors have taken the decision to close the school this summer. In addition, the historic pub, the Forest Arms, which has been closed for several years and increasingly falling into decay, has been put up for auction.'

The association's chair added: 'The character of the village has changed over the past twenty years, partly because of increased incomers moving here, partly because those people have less of a commitment to the Welsh language. Many villages like this one across the country have become a sort of dormitory for people working in the nearby towns and cities. People want to move to Carmarthen or Swansea but they can't afford the house prices and so they relocate to places like Brechfa. As a result the village is a shadow of its former self.

'What we have decided to do is save the pub. The idea is to create and develop a centre for the community. A community-run pub, cafe and restaurant. And we're also keen to attract visitors. We've spoken about running a sort of hostel for backpackers and bikers. And exploring the idea of starting a microbrewery. Other ideas for the venue could see it used as a social centre, cafe, craft centre, space for local businesses and education centre. The idea is to highlight the sort of skills and support that used to be the lifeblood of our villages but aren't there anymore.'

The association chair's name is, coincidentally, Peter Polish.

How conscious are my band of returning exiles of this changing environment that is Wales? How have they themselves been received? What are their views of the cultural and political needs of Wales?

On the coat-tails of Scotland we have approved the creation of a Welsh National Assembly, albeit as yet with very limited powers. In 1997 the Welsh public voted Yes for an Assembly by the slimmest of margins, 50.3% to 49.7%, the difference amounting to just 6,721 votes. The Welsh, after centuries of quasi-colonial rule from Westminster, still lack the confidence to believe in their own ability to govern themselves. If Westminster has a problem in getting the population to engage in politics, the situation is ten times worse in Wales.

Siôn Jobbins states in *Cambria* that 'there are two interesting books yet to be written about Wales. One is about the most important underlying feature of Welsh political life, The History of Apathy in Wales (if any historian could be bothered to write it).'

Yet, according to John Osmond of the Institute of Welsh Affairs, after the referendum result in 1997, everyone you spoke to had voted Yes.

Surely the extension of these political powers is essential, as in the absence of working-class socialism and with the disintegration of religious beliefs, there is an urgent need to create some sort of structure in Welsh lives, both to preserve Welsh values, and to provide an economy capable of sustaining the population for years to come. We certainly can't rely on Westminster.

The UK is a civilised place to live. We have a reasonable degree of freedom of speech. There are some social, political and economic benefits from belonging to a greater whole, and with most human interaction involving west to east movement into a much larger England, rather than from north to south within Wales, the two populations are naturally very intertwined. The English make up 20% of the Welsh population.

At the same time, over the centuries, Westminster, supported by the media, has paid scant attention to the individual requirements of the Welsh. We need a louder voice; we must demand a greater say, particularly in our own destiny. Yet what is the government doing: reducing the number of Welsh MPs from 40 down to 29!

But we must also stop fighting amongst ourselves. There are forever the schisms between Welsh speaker and non-Welsh speaker, between north and south, and between Cardiff and the Valleys.

The new Welsh society must not ostracise non-Welsh speakers. Non-Welsh speaking man of Gwent, Roger Banner, featured later in this book, is adamant that he feels as Welsh, if not more Welsh, than many a Welsh speaker he has encountered through his life.

And we must not forget North Wales nor the Valleys. On hearing a John Osmond speech recently given in London about the need for greater 'connectivity' in Wales, the immediate response of a successful London-based businesswoman, originally from Colwyn Bay, was to demand that we look beyond the electrification of the railway from Swansea to Paddington, to the IWA's recommendations to forge stronger transport links between Cardiff and the Valleys, and think also of opening up the rail and road avenues between the south and the north. We must not only look towards England.

Yet we must continue to be wary of the politics of Westminster. Whatever the party in power, be it Thatcher, Major, New Labour

(Tory by any other name), or the current Tory administration, the whole ethos of government seems to be people with money negotiating with people with money, to make more money – not for the population, not for the country, not even for their companies, but for themselves. In the process, the lack of stock market rules has led to financial instability, the use of foreign resources has decimated British, leave alone Welsh, industry, most of British industry (energy, transport, automotive etc.) has been sold to foreign companies, we are selling armaments to regimes with all sorts of dubious ideologies and military aims, and ploughing money into foreign aid at the expense of our education and health services.

And the population has responded, not against any of the above, but against Britain's presence in Europe. And unfortunately, the Welsh population have followed the English proletariat and the machinations of the tabloid press in voting Brexit and not Remain. It has bought into populism.

Niall Ferguson, a senior fellow at the Hoover Institution of Stanford University, California, argues in *The Times* that throughout the world, the centre-left coalition between the progressive elite and the proletariat is broken. Social democracy is dead. The elite are too liberal on immigration and too in love with multiculturalism, and the proletariat loathes both.

But our Welsh identity has much more chance of surviving if we become a recognised part of Europe as opposed to being dwarfed in a protectionist UK. With the arrival of Brexit we stand to lose a great deal of European funding which we cannot presume will be matched by Westminster, our trade will suffer if we are not part of a fairly free and open European market, and we still need to maintain a certain level of foreign immigration to provide skilled labour, particularly in the NHS, and to maintain a flourishing academic scene. Wales must be ultra defensive in its dealings within the UK, but modern and open minded in dealing with Europe and the rest of the world.

So our returning exiles have much to ponder. It is to be hoped that they have it in them to make their own contribution to the preservation of Welsh values, in terms of everyday human behaviour, their working lives, their involvement in cultural and economic activities and in the use of their political vote. Living in England, I have unfortunately never had a say in the matter.

In Search of Bright Lights

MANY EXILES LEFT Wales to broaden their horizons, often going in search of the bright lights of London. Some may find themselves forced to return home, often for family or economic reasons, yet still look back affectionately at their time in the big city, including time spent in the company of Welsh people and society, in what Byron Rogers calls 'a lunar base of Welsh exile'.

Alan Litherland

The surname Litherland is of Scouse origin, but Alan was born in Caernarfon, Gwynedd, and grew up in the little village of Criccieth on the Llŷn Peninsula.

His father came from the area around Llanrwst, in the Conwy valley, and left school at fourteen to work in the local Star grocers (part of what became the International Stores group). At the age of nineteen he became manager of their Colwyn Bay store, before moving to Criccieth, where he met Alan's mother, and thence on to Penygroes and Caernarfon.

Alan's maternal grandfather owned a newsagents in Criccieth incorporating a printing works to the rear of the building. Coincidentally, Alan's paternal grandfather and his five brothers had all also been master printers.

In 1953 Alan's parents bought the newsagents, whilst an uncle took on the printing works at the back. As a young boy, Alan clearly remembers the travel author, Jan Morris, being a regular visitor to the shop. His parents ran the shop until they retired in 1966 to Rhos on Sea near Colwyn Bay.

As an only child living in a small village, Alan found life a bit restricting, especially the rules and prejudices of a narrow, chapel-based society. By way of illustration, Alan relates iconic Welsh comedian Ryan Davies's joke about a Welshman shipwrecked on a desert island. Before he was rescued, the marooned man built two separate chapels side by side on a hill in the middle of the island.

'Why build two chapels?' asked his rescuers.

The man replied, 'Well that's the one I go to, and that's the one I'm not allowed to go to.'

In similar vein Alan speaks of a lady organist in a Methodist Chapel in Criccieth who wasn't allowed to help out at the other Methodist Chapel in the village when their organist fell sick.

Later, having returned in the early 1960s to help his father run the business, Alan also had to obey his father's instructions and only deal with certain people in the village: 'You must only buy from so-and-so's shop.'

But Alan also has fond memories of his childhood, particularly his school days and summers spent at the Urdd Gobaith Cymru (Welsh League of Youth) camp at Llangrannog in Ceredigion.

Alan has kept in touch with a group of five of his school chums over the years and, now living in Rhos on Sea near Colwyn Bay, he still contacts them on a regular basis several times a week.

The five friends all got married in the same year and have spent many subsequent reunions and holidays together with their wives.

He recalls that in their youth, before they were twenty-one, they never dared venture into any Criccieth pub for fear of 'what people might think'. Their drinking was done out of sight in the next village.

On the occasion of the wedding of one of his friends, the group were much the worse for wear from the stag night the previous evening. So at the wedding itself they limited themselves to orange juice. Word has it that his friend's mother, persuaded to believe that they were all non-drinkers, expounded to one and all the virtuousness of her 'good boys'.

But Alan grew restless in his youth, and at the age of seventeen joined the civil service in London, staying for four years in a hostel in South Kensington with fellow employees from all over the UK. He was happy to mix with everyone. He recalls the only note of dissension in his time at the hostel was the aggressive attitude two Glasgow Rangers supporters displayed towards a quiet young lad from the Falls Road area of Belfast. The Rangers supporters were soon moved on.

Alan's life in London was busy and varied. He worked in credit management for the Celanese Corporation based in Watford, finding it an exciting environment as the company gained as much as a 49% share in the market for engineering resins and plastics, and attempted to build a foothold in America.

In addition he spent two years in the police force, and his part-time occupations included being an emergency medical driver and even a bouncer at the famous 100 Jazz Club in Oxford Street.

Alan's wife and daughters were keen swimmers, his wife even a swimming coach. Alan also got involved, and became a county official with the Hertfordshire Amateur Swimming Association. He also helped out coaching patients at Stoke Mandeville, and became involved with organising the Paralympic Games at the hospital when Los Angeles refused to host them in parallel with their Olympics in 1984. The Americans, it seems, cannot muster much enthusiasm for the Paralympic version of the games, coming only seventh in the 2012 medal table compared to their second position in the Olympics themselves.

Alan also became very involved in London Welsh circles, being a regular at the centre in Gray's Inn Road, and entertainment secretary of the London Welsh football club for three years. The club at the time were flourishing with three active teams. And Alan and his ex-fellow players are still ardent supporters of the Welsh national side.

Alan is a proud Welshman and as a Welsh speaker feels sad that his Welsh 'isn't as good as it should be', these days finding it particularly hard to write in Welsh.

He has no truck with those who have moved to England and return to Wales with plums in their mouths. He remonstrated with one such acquaintance, announcing that 'your mother would be turning in her grave if she could hear your accent'.

Alan, however, married a girl from Muswell Hill and his married daughters now live in Kettering and Watford. He didn't see any point in teaching his daughters Welsh, although daughter Andrea does support the Welsh rugby and football teams and insisted on getting married in the little church on the seafront at Rhos on Sea.

Alan has in fact spent most of his life moving back and forth between London and Wales, and his memories are all about the pressure this has induced.

He had to return initially to help his father run the business, which was difficult whilst his father was still in charge. He persuaded his father to sell up, but then subsequently both his father and mother became ill, and Alan was forced into living in Wales or paying fortnightly visits over a protracted period of years.

His uncle was a rock of support and persuaded Alan to go back to London, but when he died Alan had again to return to Wales. His wife, however, loved Wales and, in fact, initially in the early 1960s settled better than Alan.

Alan's mother and father retired to Rhos on Sea many decades ago, and Alan, now divorced, lives in his mother's home, initially helping care for her there and latterly visiting her in her care home several times a week.

Alan himself is not that mobile. He has had operations to replace both hips, and now his knees are a problem. Without a car, he has had to rely on a 'fantastic' local taxi driver to ferry him to the care home and the local shops several times a week, but it all costs. Although Alan did manage to get to Cardiff for a football international in company with his old teammates from London Welsh.

Rhos on Sea is very much a retirement resort with a large immigrant population. He feels that, unlike Criccieth and Caernarfon, people don't care about their neighbours, and keep themselves to themselves. The pros and cons of the *costa geriatrica* compared to a traditional Welsh village life.

The next-door neighbours have a car, but have never offered to take Alan to see his mother, nor have they ever visited her themselves.

Alan feels that if it wasn't for his mother he'd have been 'back down south'.

And now, in her 102nd year, she has sadly passed away, and he is faced with the dilemma of whether or not to return to Watford to be nearer his two daughters.

He is not in the best of health, with his lack of mobility having led to the onset of lymphodema (a swelling of the body's tissues), in his case in the legs. Carers visit him twice a day, and although he has nothing but praise for the care given him by the Welsh NHS (the Tory government take note), he would obviously prefer to be nearer to his family.

He is still, however, very Welsh at heart. He is very much into Welsh folk music and is a regular viewer of *Noson Lawen* on S4C.

He doesn't get involved in politics, but the politicians he believes in are those who look after people and actively represent their constituency. Such a politician was Lord Dafydd Wigley, ex-president of Plaid Cymru, and fellow ex-member of the London Welsh football team. Alan is also a fan of the one-time Welsh Secretary David Jones, who lived in his constituency in Rhos on Sea, in comparison to the previous local MP Geraint Morgan, who was only likely to be seen twice a year in the constituency if you were lucky.

In the last Parliament, Alan viewed Cameron and Miliband as 'wet weeks', and Nick Clegg 'doesn't deserve to stand in the same room' as Lloyd George.

Alan is not for total Welsh independence, believing Wales isn't strong enough to cope, but voted for an Assembly as he feels it is important we have representation. He was pleased to see the views of former Education Minister Leighton Andrews receive more credence than those of then Coalition Minister

Michael Gove. But the only topic he feels really strongly about is the need for a decent transport system linking North and South Wales. There is one train a day, taking a fairly circuitous route, and the journey by road takes five hours. Consecutive governments in both London and Cardiff have only shown interest in maintaining east-west connections – that is, to and from England. How can Alan get to Cardiff for the football?

Enid Morris (née Davies)

In Porthcawl I was introduced to the enchanting ninety-year-old-Enid Morris. B She was born in Port Talbot in 1922, an only child, with a father from the nearby mining village of Bryn, and a mother from the adjacent village of Pontrhydyfen, birthplace of the actor Richard Burton.

With no hope of finding work in Wales, Enid went to college. She wanted to 'choose somewhere to enjoy herself as well' so elected to go to London.

Unfortunately it was wartime, so the college, to Enid's disappointment, was evacuated to Torquay. The students were boarded in guest houses, with three to five senior students to a room, and freshers sleeping on mattresses on the floor. Nearby Exeter and Bristol had their fair share of bombings, so most nights were spent under the beds.

'Don't tell me about romantic college days,' complains Enid.

Her father and mother had already moved to London, recommended by her mother's cousin, who was a caretaker at Jewin Chapel in the Barbican, to apply for a similar post at the Welsh Presbyterian Chapel in Charing Cross Road. Enid's mother looked after the chapel whilst her father worked in local government in Southwark Town Hall.

When Enid landed her first teaching post in Acton, she stayed with her parents in an apartment at 136 Shaftesbury Avenue, round the corner from the chapel and opposite the Cambridge Theatre. From their kitchen window they would listen to the theatre performers doing their warm up exercises in their dressing rooms before going on stage. At this point

Enid bursts into song – 'Rosalinda' from Richard Strauss's *Die Fledermaus*, performed at the Palace Theatre in 1945.

Enid admired her father more than anyone. It was from him that she acquired her love of both music and sport.

Her father was self-educated. He passed a scholarship to the local grammar school but was ashamed to wear the uniform of short trousers and blazer for fear of being called 'a sissy'. But Tom Davies made the most of his musical studies, mastering tonic sol-fa and becoming a FTSC (Fellow of the Tonic Sol-fa College). He conducted both the Bryn and Port Talbot Choral Societies to Eisteddfod success on several occasions, and led the several-hundred-strong Festival Choir at the 1934 Eisteddfod in Aberavon, backed by the London Symphony Orchestra, engaged for the week in the absence of any Welsh orchestra of note.

Enid sang in the London Welsh Choir, kept in tune by her father, although she admitted to me that she was 'not much of a singer'. However she loved the theatre, the concerts and the shows, and she and her father were regular Henry Wood Promenaders.

Like many men with their sons, Tom and Enid together became spectators of every conceivable sport. As a youngster in Wales he had lifted her over the turnstiles to see Aberavon play rugby, and she can still recite the Glamorgan cricket team of the 1930s by heart. Now in London she would stand with her father on the terraces at White Hart Lane and Highbury, watch the touring teams at Lords and the Oval, even taking in speedway at White City. And in later years Enid would queue to watch the tennis at Wimbledon, attending practically every day of the Championship fortnight.

Enid and her father also went to watch the London Welsh. Enid says she took much more delight in the rugby than in looking in shop windows.

Tom was also into politics. In the evening he would listen to the *Nine O'Clock News* on the radio, and if there was any hint of a political controversy ('hot stuff tonight', as he put it) he would head out immediately to watch the House of Commons in session, especially if Aneurin Bevan was in full voice. He was her father's hero, standing up for what he believed was right whilst making mincemeat of any opposition speaker.

Enid's mother would often persuade him to take Enid along as well, as this was the only way she could guarantee he would return at a sensible hour.

Despite being socialists, both mum and dad, and Enid, were ardent royalists. They would queue all night for any royal procession. And if Shaftesbury Avenue's traffic lights became stuck on red, they knew it must be royalty on the move, and would hurry down to the island on Cambridge Circus to watch the cavalcade as it came through, and wave to the royals inside their cars. Enid was convinced her mother expected the King to stop the car, wind down the window and ask, 'How are you today, Mrs Davies?'

They obviously became fully involved in London Welsh chapel society. In true Welsh fashion, Enid's mother worshipped at the Presbyterian Chapel in the Charing Cross Road, but her dad on some Sundays attended a different denomination, the Baptist Chapel in Castle Street. He did later, however, become a deacon and elder at Charing Cross Road.

Tom Davies was also a regular visitor to Griff's Welsh bookshop just off the Charing Cross Road, where the London Welsh chapelgoers would congregate for coffee and a good old 'chinwag' about politics, rugby and things Welsh.

Enid's mum and dad always spoke Welsh to each other but English to Enid. Enid, however, had plenty of opportunity to converse in Welsh as most chapel activities were conducted through the medium of the Welsh language. Enid observed that in chapel even those with the strongest Cockney accents sounded as if they came from Aberystwyth when conversing in their mother tongue. She also came to the conclusion later that, in fact, back home in Wales not so many people were speaking Welsh.

Enid feels the Welsh are more homely – 'we are as we are'. She had lots of English friends, and held nothing against them, but felt they didn't have the warmth of the Welsh. We have 'the gift of the gab.' Travelling on the Underground, it didn't take her father two minutes to strike up a conversation, and in the end he had everybody talking.

Holidays were always taken back in Wales. Her parents would have a week in Porthcawl, and she and her father would also take in the National Eisteddfod, her mother declining to attend, claiming that she had had enough of the Eisteddfod and its rain.

After her father and mother retired to Wales, Enid continued to teach in London and the South East, initially living in Pinner whilst teaching in Wembley, ('Middlesex was a little bit more refined than Acton'), then later becoming a deputy headmistress in Surrey, living in 'digs' at the house of an ex-Grenadier Guardsman, the head gardener on the West Horsley Estate, once occupied by Carew Raleigh, son of Sir Walter.

She would still travel into central London to attend chapel in Charing Cross on a Sunday, followed by even more Welsh singing at Speaker's Corner in Hyde Park and tea at Lyons Corner House on Marble Arch, before heading off home.

But her father was missing her and was keen for her to return to Wales. And Enid didn't mind. She had spent all her lengthy school holidays in South Wales, and had kept in touch with friends, 'a big jolly crowd', many of whom had also spent time in London. And there was still the cricket and the rugby, and the occasional concerts at the Brangwyn Hall and St David's Hall.

Enid had always enjoyed the company of men, but wasn't in a hurry to get married. Yet on returning to Wales she did get married, to her second cousin, Eirwyn, who had 'quite a good job' as a clerk, first on the council and then with the steel company.

Eirwyn didn't want to be uprooted from Wales, so in Wales Enid stayed, claiming never to have regretted leaving London, whilst adding wistfully, 'It's nicer in a way in Wales. If you are Welsh, you are Welsh. But in London you were Welsh too, but more cosmopolitan.'

The Good Life

WE MUSTN'T UNDERVALUE what the land of Wales has to offer. The English, even though most can't tell one end of Wales from the other, continue to regale and ridicule us with jokes about rain and sheep. But several of my fellow exiles decided to return to Wales specifically because of the environment, the countryside, the mountains and the coast, together with the relaxed pace of life on offer.

And with the removal of the heavy industry that was at one time the heartbeat of Wales, this environment has been further improved. In Llanelli, for example, where there once stood a promenade of steelworks, we now have the Millennium Coastal Path, described as 'a tranquil green corridor offering superb views of the Gower', with its traffic-free cycle and footpath, bird sanctuary, championship links golf course, a marina at Burry Port and a country park in Pembrey.

To enter Ebbw Vale, one once had to drive through the black hole that was the enormous Steel Company of Wales works. This was transformed in 1992 for the Garden Festival of Wales, and is now a popular shopping centre and tourist attraction, with a fishing lake, owl sanctuary, gym, a festival church surrounded by sculptures, and an adventure playground with the UK's longest supertubing run.

Cardiff and Swansea docks have also seen residential and retail redevelopment, incorporating major exhibition and entertainment venues such as the Millennium Centre, Wales's answer to the Sydney Opera House.

Not that our returning exiles in the seclusion of their rural and suburban retreats have need for such post-industrial transformations. For the most part, the refurbishment of most town centres has been particularly badly planned, as is true of most of the UK, but the lives of these exiles are mainly spent in relaxed, scenic environments outside of such urban developments.

Wales has the added benefit of a much lower cost of living, particularly in relation to the price of housing. One can either afford a considerably larger property or pocket several hundred thousand pounds to more easily enjoy one's retirement.

These returning exiles feel they could have settled in similar spots across the length and breadth of the UK, but family connections and a certain, typically Welsh, nostalgia for their childhood haunts has brought them home to Wales. But the attraction is mainly the result of family and place, not of community.

They are apolitical or anti-politics. Their need is for the freedom to get on with and enjoy their lives, and they feel that the generally civilised attitude of most of the UK's society offers such an opportunity. Government just gets in the way.

They are either non-Welsh speakers who see themselves as British more than Welsh, or Welsh speakers as a simple matter of fact and heredity rather than political choice.

They are happy with their lot in retirement.

Geoff Griffiths

Ex-Llanelli Grammarian, Geoff Griffiths, and his English wife, Julia, live in a large detached house above the Llanelli village of Felinfoel, overlooking on the one side the local beauty spot of Swiss Valley, and on the other the expanse of Carmarthen Bay and the Gower Peninsula.

Geoff is a self-confessed recluse. He watches a lot of television, spends time reading, and dabbles in the stock market online. At his age he values peace and quiet away from the rat race. He is happy to chill out.

He plays the occasional game of golf, though hasn't renewed his club membership, even though the course on the Gower provides 'millionaire's golf': a round of golf with the course to yourself, yet at half the price of London and the South East.

London Welsh AFC, circa 1959. Alan Litherland, from Criccieth, is the last on the right in the back row.

Enid Morris of Port Talbot outside Charing Cross Chapel, London.

Geoff and Julia Griffiths outside Parc y Scarlets.

Geoff and Julia's house in Llanelli's Swiss Valley.

Llanelli from the Gower Golf Club's 6th green.

Tudor Lloyd Thomas, Lord Griffiths, Peter Lane and the author prior to a Llanelli Boys Grammar School and Graig Comprehensive Former Pupils' Dinner.

Tony Jenkins and the author prior to the alternative Former Pupils' Dinner.

Peter and Sandra Williams with Scarlet the Second outside their Llanelli Swiss Valley home.

The Gower from Carmarthenshire, near Tony and Catriona Jenkins's home.

The once-iconic pink pavilion, and the usual rain, at the National Eisteddfod, Llantwit Major 2012.

Cowbridge choir, Côr Meibion Y Machlud, with Llew Thomas second left in the back row, alongside JPR Williams.

(with thanks to Alan Moss, photographer)

St Illtyd's Church, Llantwit Major.

(painting by Gill Daniels)

Roger and Margaret Banner's house, near Monmouth.

The view from Roger and Margaret's house.

Roger Banner and his two sons.

Gillian, from Newport, receiving her master's degree.

Gillian and her sister Ceri.

Richard and Mary Davies on their smallholding in Penybont, Powys.

Richard with the lambs.

Huw Jones of Pontarddulais.

Huw and Eira Jones on holiday.

Cledwyn and Suzanne Davies and family before his skydive.

Cledwyn's 65th birthday skydive.

(Skydive Hibaldstow)

Rhian Jones at a London Welsh reception for the 2013 British and Irish Lions.

Rhian and her two brothers supporting the Swans at the Liberty Stadium.

Rhian in Welsh dress at Tŷ Tawe,
Swansea's Welsh Language Centre.

Iain Richards of Blackwood.

Blackwood's Chartist Bridge and statue to honour the Chartists' march to Newport in 1839.

(with permission of Caerphilly Borough Council)

Blackwood's Velvet Coalmine Festival, 2015.

He occasionally goes to Parc y Scarlets, but is just as happy watching rugby indoors, out of the cold, on television, helped by a knowledgeable commentary, as opposed to 'listening to one-eyed, apoplectic neanderthals shouting at the referee'.

The single evidence of his earlier competitiveness is his passion for playing bridge in Welsh Bridge Union tournaments which he describes as a bit more exacting than 'golf club bridge'.

Geoff and Julia looked within a twenty-mile radius for the right house and discovered the best houses were to be found in Llanelli. They bought just at the right time at the turn of the millennium. They paid about half the price a similar house would have cost them in their previous location in Kent, and by 2012 it was worth about two-and-a-half times the original price they paid.

The general cost of living is also much lower, most noticeably reflected in the price of a pint of beer, but given the lower average wage, possibly not appreciated as much by the locals.

And as far as the retail offer is concerned, one town is very much like another. They all have their Currys and Frankie & Bennys. Geoff doesn't venture into town very often anyway; just for Asda, the market, the dentist and the bank.

Ten miles out of Dartford you were in beautiful scenery. But according to Julia, the Welsh countryside is wilder, less cultivated, more special, and less congested with traffic. There is also the sea and the coastal path. And in Dartford they had long ceased to utilise the many benefits that London had to offer.

The one remaining drawback to their move to West Wales is the need to give support to their daughter, recently widowed, still living in Kent.

Julia has become well used to Llanelli and Wales over the years, with countless holidays and visits to Geoff's mum.

She appreciates the Welsh sense of humour, finding it a touch on the black side. This brings to mind a joke told me recently by a Welsh learner, about a husband who suffered a heart attack while picking out a cabbage from his allotment for the family Sunday dinner.

'How did you cope?' a neighbour asked of the wife.

'Oh there wasn't a problem,' replied the wife, 'I just opened a tin of peas.'

Julia hails from Cheshire, but has realised that South Wales Man has a significantly greater nostalgia for times and places past, a need to hold on tightly to every aspect of earlier childhood. Geoff speaks lovingly of being part of boyhood gangs climbing the trees in Stradey Woods, of visits to Llanelli's iconic indoor market, of the learning buzz he experienced whilst at the grammar school, of playing tennis for the county, of being a drummer in a rock and roll band, of his favourite pubs and of watching the Scarlets play at Stradey Park.

He claims such elements of nostalgia are to be found amongst many Welsh people living in England. Yet after twelve years back in Llanelli he wonders what the fuss was about. When he first returned he was so enthusiastic about things. But this slowly wears away, and he now takes things far more for granted.

And as a teenager Geoff couldn't wait to 'escape' from Llanelli. He liked school but it was a passport to better things. His first priority was self-improvement, to earn a good living and see a bit of the world, in the manner that the cinema often portrays film characters leaving small town America.

Geoff felt he was both competitive and anarchic. A smoker who was definitely not prefect material. He played county-standard tennis and was a drummer in the Corncrackers rock band led by Deke Leonard, later to become famous as the frontman of the rock bands Man and Iceberg.

Geoff claims he became a drummer because of his total inability to sing. He recounts the tale of his primary school teacher begging him to mime when his school class were asked to form a choir for a local church's Christmas celebrations.

Llanelli offered him nothing on a professional level but where he ended up living was purely down to circumstance. He wanted to go to university and gained a place at Bristol, where he met his wife, Julia. Subsequently the University of Surrey offered him a master's degree in spectroscopy, and scientific job opportunities were forthcoming from Boots in Nottingham and Wellcome in Dartford. The Dartford position seemed more interesting and offered £50 more with a starting salary worth the princely sum of £1,200. 'It just happened to be Dartford.'

With responsibility for a wife and family Geoff must have become less of a rebel and progressed at Wellcome in what he describes as 'a job for life'. Julia also made good progress teaching English, becoming deputy head of the local grammar school at the early age of twenty-six and acquiring an MA from the University of London.

The anarchic side of Geoff quite liked being Welsh in England, being different, with a definite identity. He liked to 'take the piss' when we won at rugby (we did more frequently in those days) just like the Aussies do at cricket. He feels the English see themselves as the master race, so being Welsh he likes to pull them down.

Over time, as he became successful in a 'proper job', Geoff developed more feelings of nostalgia for his Welsh roots, and in retirement he now looks for the quiet life away from the rat race.

But he thinks he would have felt the same if he had been born in Yorkshire. He is not in love with life in a Welsh community, it just happens to be his community, one with which he is familiar. He is done with partying. He and Julia are happy to have a small circle of friends, and many are exiles or exiles like Geoff who have returned to Wales.

Politically Geoff is more British than Welsh. His background closely resembles my own. His father was a steel company foreman, and like my own father, who worked in the steel company's offices, he was management and therefore Tory by inclination, even in a Labour hotbed like Llanelli. He also ran a pub, just as my father spent many hours helping in his parents' hostelry.

Geoff's politics show similar traits, believing the last Labour government destroyed the economy. But a vote for the Conservatives would be a wasted vote in Llanelli, so he is inclined to favour UKIP, although he is not anti-immigration, believing that 'the world is changing' and that immigrants are only doing work the indigenous population are too lazy to perform.

Geoff has no time for the Welsh Assembly, seeing the duplication of government as costing money. Similarly the duplication of official forms and road signs in both Welsh and English is a waste of money that could be better spent in other ways. On the other hand he thinks it excellent that children are learning Welsh in schools. The more languages you speak the better.

Geoff favours a civilised existence and believes the UK offers this. On the census form he is British. Nationalism and religion only get in the way. He is actually apolitical, a believer in having the freedom to do whatever takes your fancy.

Yet there is still a slightly anarchic streak evident in his parting remark: 'I made my money in England, so I've brought it back to Wales to spend it.'

Peter Lane

Another ex-Llanelli Grammarian Peter Lane and his English wife Margaret live in a large and splendid Edwardian house on a hill above the pleasant village of Oystermouth, just outside Swansea, on the fringe of the Gower Peninsula overlooking the attractive crescent that is Swansea Bay.

Peter can see the bay through the window as he sits and works each day, looking out at the rain. 'What else would you want?'

Recent generations of his family hailed from Swansea, although his father had some original English (East London) antecedents. Peter's grandmother might have spoken Welsh, but he would not describe either his father's or mother's family as Welsh-speaking.

His father managed various tinplate works, first in Swansea, then Port Talbot, and finally in 1955, at Trostre in Llanelli. It was at this time that Peter moved from Neath Grammar School to join me at Llanelli Grammar School.

He found the school very disjointed and dysfunctional. For more than ten years its location was split between two separate sites, miles apart at different ends of the town. 'Why couldn't Carmarthen County Council afford to build one school? Ridiculous!'

He also found that 'in school you never knew whether a teacher was going to reprimand you in Welsh or in English.' Peter perceived there to be an elitist element in the school, with Welsh speakers being more favoured by the staff, their achievements more acknowledged. 'You were the bee's knees if you could recite poetry in Welsh.'

His local area of Bryn had a similar conflicting duality, situated as it was between the Welsh-speaking villages of Hendy and Llangennech and the English-speaking town centre.

He was aware from the media of lots of news about what Wales didn't have. It gave him a feeling that Wales was being treated as a second class citizen. This didn't, however, make him more patriotic. 'I supported Welsh rugby, and that was about it.'

In his time at Cambridge studying for a degree in chemistry, he was also conscious of an attitude of mind amongst fellow students which assumed that all things English were better. He again saw this as just a minor problem. 'You could try to be very Welsh, or not bother. I just didn't bother. I didn't mix with a very elitist group, just bright boys from working-class backgrounds. It didn't matter.

'I think of Wales as a nice country, a nice place, but I wouldn't take up arms to defend it.'

His career took him firstly, for four years, to Merseyside, working for Unilever, who subsequently moved him to Blackfriars in London to work as a statistics manager in Van den Bergh's market research department.

When Van den Bergh moved to Burgess Hill, Peter took the opportunity of an offer from IDV in Harlow, the company even paying for him to move house. He stayed for seven years. He lived in Woodford, later in Chingford, and it was here at the local bridge club that he met his wife, Margaret, also working as a statistician, at the Government Statistical Service.

Peter and Margaret visited his parents and sister in Swansea quite often, for 'family things' like weddings and anniversaries. They quite fancied the area and bought a flat in Langland Bay which they encouraged his parents to use whilst they were finding a place of their own. Peter and Margaret then alternated staying in the flat with leasing it as a holiday let.

Both their careers were going through a static phase, so when the owner of the letting company died, they bought the business and moved down to Swansea.

Peter sees the Gower and Swansea Bay as 'an incredibly nice place to live', although it could be anywhere really. Somerset and Devon would probably be just as nice, it just happens he has family in South Wales.

Being near the sea is always pleasant. Oystermouth is a perfect little village with interesting local rather than chain-store businesses, beaches and countryside nearby, restaurants and a tennis club just up the road, and the urban benefits of Swansea and Cardiff only ten and forty minutes away.

With Margaret's father passing away, they have also bought an apartment in Chingford and they now alternate between the two locations.

They are huge opera buffs, but Peter finds it just as easy, if not easier, to visit the opera in Cardiff when in Swansea than to attend the London Coliseum when in London.

Swansea may have segments of its population on benefits and drugs, but Peter's end of town is well looked after and reasonably affluent. Likewise, Chingford has a more upper-middle class character than not-too-far-away Leyton or Walthamstow.

Earlier I suggested that historically the exclusion of the Welsh and their language from positions of authority by the English meant that to get on in life required acquiring the affectations of the English, talking 'posh' and acting as if one owned the world.

Today's Swansea has its own middle class just like Chingford. The only difference identified by Peter is that one speaks with a

Welsh, the other with a North-London accent. And the middle class of Chingford are equally as artisan, not necessarily 'old school'. The Western world has become more democratic and cosmopolitan. (Even if covertly, I suggest that the class system still operates, with David Cameron's cabinet in the last Tory government being as full of old Etonians as was Macmillan's in 1960).

The new cosmopolitan world isn't, however, totally to Peter's liking. He sees the globalisation of US culture as the spreading of the lowest common denominator. Swansea now has better restaurants (a UK rather than a Welsh development), it has a subsidised Taliesin Arts Centre on the Singleton university campus and two independent cinemas, but the mainstream fodder is still rubbish blockbusters and burgers from the States. You visit quaint and interesting countries, then the next time you go, 'there's a bloody McDonald's!'

One of the reasons Peter prefers the opera in Cardiff to the Coliseum is that London has become so much more of a fairground on a Saturday night than of old.

He is also happy to see the growth of Welsh culture, and the encouragement of an awareness of the repression and struggles of history, but a Welsh identity should be modern and not just reflect archaic happenings. It shouldn't just be alright 'as long as we beat the English'.

He believes it is good for the kids to learn the Welsh language; an encouraging first step towards becoming multilingual. And Welsh culture is becoming better at welcoming newcomers into its fold. One of the professors at Swansea University, for example, who hails from the Potteries, has a daughter in *Pobol Y Cwm*.

It is also good for dual road signs to announce that you are in Wales, but they don't need to tell you to slow down in Welsh. Such a bilingual facility should be available, but it is a complete waste of money to translate everything, especially if it's the same word differently spelt. Suggests Peter, 'If you spoke to an official in Welsh, even just saying *bore da*, he'd probably fall off his chair.'

Peter would be quite happy with a federal UK. After all, such a structure exists in both the USA and Germany. And he likes to watch regional TV programmes dependent on where he is at the time. 'They reflect things going on around you.' And unlike yours truly, he not only feels that there is sufficient Welsh television, but that Wales has an increasing presence on national television.

'The worm has turned. There was Huw Wheldon, now we have Huw Edwards and John Humphrys. Dylan Thomas is wonderful. There are several production companies in Wales. And *Escape to the Country* comes to Wales quite a lot, saying "What a nice place to live".'

He sees the actual problem in Wales as 'the really inefficient Assembly'.

While Peter sees Wales as a second-class country, hard done by by Westminster, he feels the current situation is also something of our own making. The Welsh Development Agency, he felt, had the wrong approach, introducing schemes to train people for a proliferation of meaningless government positions, rather than maximising the availability of jobs by encouraging the growth of small businesses. Cardiff has become a huge bureaucracy of government systems focused exclusively on promoting party political dogma.

Peter still keeps active on the business front and is currently helping market a new low-energy cooker. He also tendered to the Welsh Assembly for a market-research project into the value-added market for natural Welsh produce. His colleague was both the author of three books about Welsh food, and a Welsh speaker. The tender was however won by the consultancy arm of an Edinburgh estate agent who knew nothing about the background to the project. Peter found the depth of bureaucracy surrounding the pitch quite amazing.

In contrast, many of my teacher friends have spoken in the past about the 'closed shop' that is South Wales when applying for teaching posts back home. I suggest that neither nepotism nor bureaucracy can be said to be very positive attributes, whether in Labour Wales or Tory Westminster.

Peter has moved a little more to the left since his days as a Tory candidate in a mock school election, although in the last analysis he saw party politics at the time of our discussion as 'a bit absurd. There isn't a left or a right at the moment.'

And despite the low regard the English have for Wales, he also doesn't see the personalities of the people as that different.

Peter identifies two different types of Welshman. The mass of the Welsh in the Valleys, and Cardiff and Swansea, really migrated there from the rest of the country. They are from the same stock as the rest of the UK.

He sees the urban Welsh as reasonably unprejudiced, fairly open, garrulous, friendly to anybody.

The rural more indigenous Welsh are also friendly, but more guarded and not quite so open.

He would include Llanelli townsfolk within this category. Despite being an industrial town it has closer links to Wales's agricultural and cultural past. The population are friendly and kind to people, but more inward, less overt, more closed.

According to Peter, if you asked a Llanelli man for directions to Newcastle Emlyn, his immediate response would be 'What do you want to go there for?'

The often-made claim that the rural Welsh switch to speaking Welsh if an Englishman walks in the room he sees as truth, not myth, and probably with good reason. He recognises that English marauders may have left their mark.

The English are even more of a mixed race, of many different nationalities. The Welsh may be more welcoming to immigrants on a small scale, but he can understand the growth of antagonism in places like Bradford or Leicester where there has been a much more conspicuous influx of newcomers of a different race and religion, many not even speaking the language of the host nation.

But even excluding the influx of such different nationalities, English Northerners and Southerners would also not necessarily consider themselves part of the same group.

According to Peter, 'most people are alright'. In London people talk all the time, it is a myth that they keep themselves to themselves.

And northern England is an industrial environment similar to Wales, a socialist-leaning, rent-paying crowd, rather than land-owning gentry; the home of nonconformity and the co-operative movement. Seeing themselves as more open and friendly than those 'down south'.

So my own long-held belief that life and people are better to the west of Offa's Dyke, Peter sees as an example of the syndrome of 'the grass always being greener on the other side of the fence'. He is, however, very happy and content living on that other side of the fence.

Llew Thomas

David Llewelyn (Llew) Thomas was born in Harrow, Middlesex, in 1942, the son of a couple from Trisant near Devil's Bridge just outside Aberystwyth, who a year earlier had moved to London in search of work. His father, originally a farm labourer, worked on the roads. His mother had been in service.

Llew had a completely Welsh upbringing, speaking Welsh rather than English, both at home and in chapel, first in Wembley and later in Harrow. He was also a regular at the London Welsh Centre, performing recitations at local eisteddfodau and singing with the London Welsh Male Voice Choir.

His father and mother hadn't themselves visited the centre too often, the cost of the rail fare into London being a major deterrent.

It was at the centre, however, that Llew met his wife, Gill, the daughter of a miner from Seven Sisters in the Dulais valley, a tributary of the River Neath. Gill was a primary school teacher, and is also a Welsh speaker.

Throughout his life, Llew has worked hard to better himself. Beginning as a trainee butcher at the age of seventeen, he joined Rotaprint in Harrow, where he became an instructor teaching people how to operate the print machines. He then progressed to become print manager and then telecoms manager for Joe Lyons, before finally setting up his own telecom consultancy.

His son, Huw, has also become a very successful accountant, supporting the old adage that the fortunes of a family can quite easily reverse across a couple of generations.

Llew invested wisely in a house in a desirable road in Harrow in the early 1970s, which was sold at a considerable profit in 1987 in order for Llew and Gill to move out to a village near Whipsnade and buy a property with an acre of land for the children's pony. Both Gill and their children were keen riders. A cousin is in fact a National Hunt trainer.

Very sadly, daughter Cathryn was killed in a road accident at the tender age of fourteen.

Son Huw progressed from Dunstable Comprehensive to Cambridge, before training as an accountant.

Huw speaks Welsh, although, according to his father, this was not forced on him. But it does mean that both father and son have mastered our language despite being born and bred in London. Quite an achievement, although it also demonstrates how much easier is the preservation of the language when both parents possess the mother tongue.

In retirement, Llew and Gill wanted to downsize to a less rural location. Also, whilst the neighbours in their five-house hamlet were friendly enough ('they had to be, in such a small community'), Dunstable was 'dead, empty and scruffy'.

They chose Wales for its scenery (East Anglia was too flat), a lower cost of living and because of their roots. They looked at Pembrokeshire, the Gower Peninsula and then chose Llantwit Major, in the Vale of Glamorgan. The rural farmland was like the Wales Llew knew from countless childhood holidays on the farm near Aberystwyth. Their cottage has lovely views of the Bristol Channel. The location is at the same time more urban than their Bedfordshire village. The shops are open and busy, unlike Dunstable with its charity shops, and there are three supermarkets and five pubs within walking distance. Most important in retirement.

Cardiff also provides the occasional, possibly monthly, opportunity to visit larger shops and the theatre, along with the chance to watch Wales at the Millennium (renamed Principality) Stadium, although Llew found this a bit of a nightmare, 'people passing you all the time with trays of beer'.

In comparison Dunstable, in Bedfordshire, had far less to offer and visiting London was too much of an effort.

Llew's roots are Welsh and the Welsh language. But his parents were not at all nationalistic. They happened to be Welsh and to speak Welsh. It was just 'a matter of fact'.

It is similar with Llew. He sings in a local Cowbridge choir, Meibion y Machlud, and speaks Welsh during rehearsals. (JPR Williams is a fellow chorister, and is also learning Welsh). Llew and Gill also visit the Royal Welsh Show, and the National Eisteddfod, when it is based in South Wales every other year. But they didn't specifically seek out a Welsh-speaking area in which to retire, and whilst being a Welsh speaker, Gill doesn't feel encouraged to converse in the language. And even with a base in South Wales they haven't really made a great effort to keep more in touch with their extended families.

Their Llantwit neighbours are friendly and were very helpful when they first moved into the area. But Llew also felt 'neighbours were OK' when a child in Harrow. On an individual level, he has no gripe with the English; it is on a national level that his antagonism surfaces.

Yet Llew's politics are really quite ambivalent. He hates the English nation 'with a vengeance' for their treatment of the Welsh throughout history. And even in the present day he feels that Westminster has used Wales as a guinea pig for such developments as council tax revaluation and the analog/digital changeover, yet can't even agree to provide us with a second three-lane motorway. He feels the Welsh as a nation are more principled.

The national media he sees as only featuring Wales if there

has been a murder, and Wales has only the *Western Mail* to offer as an alternative.

But whilst being proud to be Welsh he still considers himself British, even pro-UKIP, believes Wales does not to have the money to become independent and considers the Welsh Assembly to be the worst idea we've ever had. Welsh politicians have learnt from their English counterparts as to what they can get away with in politics.

In the last analysis Llew is anti-politics. 'Politics in total should be banned.' He finds it incredible that the government of his small and rural local area is handled by as many as five separate levels of administration: the town council; the Vale of Glamorgan Council; the Welsh Assembly; the Westminster Government and the European Parliament, which he suggests is both expensive and tantamount to 'a police state'.

Yet despite his ranting, Llew and Gill are still more than happy to ignore the machinations of the outside political world and enjoy the good life in their idyllic rural retreat in the beautiful Vale of Glamorgan.

Community

THERE ARE OTHERS who have returned to Wales not only to be closer to their families and friends, but who have in addition returned to experience the broader sense of community they feel exists in Welsh compared to English neighbourhoods, especially in comparison to those in the south east of England.

They consider such community spirit results in a far closer-knit society with more friendly socialising and a higher level of helpfulness and trust between neighbours.

Although not necessarily Welsh speakers, they are more conscious of Welsh culture and have always imagined returning 'home' to their roots at some stage in their lives. They are proud to be Welsh and recognise the need for Wales to improve its economic lot within the United Kingdom. As with most of my returning exiles, this doesn't mean, however, that they approve of what the National Assembly in Cardiff has achieved, or failed to achieve.

The timing of their return is a question of circumstance. Some have returned a decade or more later than anticipated as a result of employment commitments or opportunities. Others have been forced to return much earlier because of a lack of employment and the higher cost of living that is today's London and southern England, or in one instance in an attempt to improve the educational progress of their offspring.

Gillian

Most Welsh exiles have migrated to England, in particular to the South East, in search of a livelihood. At one time practically every teacher and milkman in London was Welsh. The 'staff room' had become 'the Taff room', and my English friends always speak lovingly of their schooldays, being taught rugby by a 'hard but fair' Welsh PE teacher.

But times have changed, and whilst jobs still abound in the UK capital, the cost of living, and particularly housing, has escalated out of all proportion, and the Welsh have been driven to return to their homeland, in search of a more economical lifestyle, helped by their families.

I first met Gillian at a Welsh learners' class at London's Grays Inn Road during the mid-noughties. She was also a member of the London Welsh Chorale, a London Welsh mixed choir. Whilst she was really enjoying life, and was often the life and soul of the party, Gillian herself is not sure, whether, coming to London from Newport as a very young twenty-year-old, she would have survived its vast anonymity without her involvement in the London Welsh Centre. She was told about its choirs in advance, and having arrived in London in the November, she had by the January already joined the London Welsh Chorale.

A graduate in biochemical science from the University of Coventry, she had previously worked as a biologist in the Heath Hospital laboratories in Cardiff. When her project came to an end, she sought work in London, following her sister to the UK capital.

She spent ten years working at the London School of Hygiene and Tropical Medicine, whilst simultaneously studying part time for a master's degree in molecular microbiology. With the completion of her degree, her work at the school of medicine also came to an end, and whilst she was putting the finishing touches to her thesis, she moved in with her sister and brother in law, commuting into London from Harpenden in Hertfordshire. To make ends meet she worked in the offices and bar of the London Welsh Centre, but this barely met the costs of the expensive commute from Harpenden.

So Gillian has returned to Newport, initially living with her parents as she could only find short-term fixed-contract work, firstly as a scientist, subsequently as a trainee teacher. But she has now embarked on a new career as a fully-qualified special needs teaching assistant, and has obtained a full-time position at a comprehensive in Chepstow. Every school class between the age of eleven and sixteen has special-needs children integrated into the normal class, receiving the same education, but with specialised teaching for some of their work.

As a consequence of her new full-time occupation, Gillian has both been able to afford a car, and, helped by monies handed down on the death of her grandmother, bought her own house. Although she still feels the need to qualify as a child minder to further supplement her income.

Gillian has always said that she would have inevitably eventually returned home to Wales, in search of both her family and community roots. And in buying a house she has also laid down roots of her own, and the partygoer of old now spends much of her time looking after and busily decorating her new acquisition. She even has two little cats, Vivien and Leigh.

Several of her friends from the choir have followed the same path, transferring their jobs to Wales, either to get married or to return to their families. Gillian's sister now lives in Usk and Gillian pops in from Chepstow after school about twice a week to see her and her children.

Despite coming from Newport in south-east Wales, quite close to the English border, Gillian also wants to engage in Welsh culture, and she sees this as an important element of her identity within both her family and her community.

She didn't learn Welsh in school. Apparently it ceased to be compulsory after the 1960s. But her grandparents on her mother's side were farmers from Machynlleth, and although the language was lost when the family moved down to the South Wales Valleys, Gillian still experienced her grandfather speaking Welsh when she visited his farm in the Vale of Glamorgan, and enjoyed sampling their Welsh way of life, staying on the farm, with its traditional afternoon teas and evening sing songs. She also spent much time with her cousins, who unlike her were learning Welsh in school.

She has continued her Welsh lessons in Newport, even passing her GCSE, and has found more Welsh being spoken in the town than she anticipated. There is a Welsh school, a Welsh chapel, and *Merched y Wawr*, a Welsh-language version of the Women's Institute.

She has also joined a choir, Côr Y Dreigiau, and was enlisted into the National Eisteddfod Choir for the 2016 Eisteddfod in Abergavenny, which in addition encouraged her to practise her Welsh with some of her fellow choristers.

She thinks the Welsh are passionate about their own culture, and in an interesting take, feels that, in contrast, the people of England, the land that brought us Shakespeare and Dickens, have no equivalent folk culture. Her image of popular English culture relates only to football hooligans and celebrity television, and she sees London, with all its immigrants and tourists, as no longer being representative of the greater England.

Prior to experiencing London at first hand, her image of the southern English was all snobbery and public schools, and she imagined that towns in the north of England were probably closer to Wales in the character of their people. But her work environment turned out to be extremely multicultural, and the only 'typically' English she encountered were the upmarket businessmen in city pubs who 'took the mick' out of her accent.

Gillian enjoyed her time in London but has had no regrets about returning to Wales. Life feels safer. You can talk to people, a random person in a shop, a complete stranger, without them thinking you are mad.

In Newport, she is friendly with her next-door neighbours, a couple in their early fifties.

'In London you wouldn't even talk to your neighbours.

'Wales is more relaxed. You have time to do things. You are home by four not seven or eight o'clock. In London, rather than go home to change, you'd go straight out for the evening.'

Wales is also cleaner, has less pollution and better air. Gillian wasn't the only returning exile to claim this, even though I find it in sharp contrast to my recall of the belching steelworks that represented Llanelli's promenade during my formative years.

Newport has obviously changed since her childhood. When she was in her late teens, she felt the centre was fine, with its pubs and clubs, and an attendant police van to keep trouble to a minimum. Over time, however, the city has, like many other places in post-industrial Britain, seen some urban decline. Unemployment is high since the closure of the main part of the huge Llanwern steelworks, and there are lots of people living on benefits in the various council estates. But if any area has a rough reputation you just don't go there. Gillian claims never to have been scared anywhere in the world. She feels safe.

She has tended to shop in a sizeable retail park closer to her home rather than use the city centre, and her social life has partly focussed on the brighter lights of Cardiff.

But at the same time Gillian feels that Newport isn't as bad as it is sometimes portrayed in the press. There has recently been considerable redevelopment: a new shopping precinct, Friar's Walk, the Riverside Theatre complex, and the site of the old Llanwern steelworks is now a wetlands bird sanctuary. And it has a station on the main line to Paddington, and two airports within 45 minutes' drive.

In summary, she describes it as a 'nice' place to live, and adds that, after all, 'home is where the heart is'.

She has never given a second thought about her return to Wales. According to the census she is Welsh and not British, and she was persuaded by a member of Plaid Cymru, during a visit to the National Eisteddfod, to join the party. She believes that Wales, like Scotland and Northern Ireland, should not be giving over their resources to the government in Westminster. Wales must preserve its language and its land. She was disappointed with Brexit as she believes we need EU money, although she is also aware that EU rules are in danger of wrecking Welsh farming.

Whilst not wishing to be active politically, as an individual she is pro-Plaid Cymru and Welsh independence, but doesn't imagine a definitive independent or even federal state will happen in her lifetime.

Anthony (Tony) Jenkins

Tony and Catriona Jenkins have homes in Twickenham, Middlesex and Pwll, Llanelli. They have succeeded in combining their love of the 'bright lights' of London with the ability to escape the bustle, the traffic and the planes for the 'good life' of a second more secluded, more rural retreat.

Believe it or not, just after the millennium, their choice of a retirement retreat rested between Pwll and Provence. They were booked to go on a holiday to Provence to investigate the French housing market, but at the same time Tony's mam was regularly sending them details of properties in Llanelli. Then about two weeks before their holiday, they visited Llanelli for the christening of Tony's sister's first grandchild, and ended up buying a house, even before sampling the delights of southern France.

They had always found Llanelli a nice place to visit, and years earlier, when enjoying the sun on Llanelli beach during Catriona's pregnancy, they had jokingly talked of what a lovely place it would be to return to. And the sitting room in their house in Pwll continues to provide them with similarly gorgeous views of the Gower and the Burry Estuary on a daily basis. Catriona also describes to me how she is immediately conscious of the freshness of the sea air every time they alight from the train at Llanelli station. Although again I must confess this didn't match the steelwork smoke I recall from my own childhood.

Tony admits that if forced to choose between their two abodes he would still settle for the restaurants, theatres and sporting arenas of London, although he's not sure Catriona would make the same choice.

And the appeal of Llanelli is more than just the 'good life'; for both of them it also provides a much needed broader sense of community.

Tony grew up in a close-knit Welsh family. His mother was born in Llanelli's New Dock area, but moved to New Zealand Street, near Stradey Park, at the age of eleven. Even in her later years, she talked of how the short ten-minute walk to the town centre used to take her hours as she stopped to talk to every passerby.

Tony's father was a Welsh speaker, and Tony recalls Welsh regularly being spoken when visiting his grandparents in Bynea every Tuesday. Tony studied Welsh as a foreign language for O-level, and also sang in All Saints Church choir, whilst his father was a member of Côr Meibion Llanelli.

Since returning to Llanelli, Tony has loved meeting up regularly with his old school friends, many of whom have never left Llanelli. Even in London his close circle of friends are mainly of Welsh origin, and he is forever telling me about someone he has met who has connections with our joint early lives in Llanelli. He is a one-man networking organisation. He even keeps in touch with his parents' old neighbours in New Zealand Street.

And when holidaying abroad he claims that 'once you meet someone Welsh, you spend the rest of your holiday with them.'

In Pwll, he and Catriona have got to know their neighbours really well. In Twickenham the neighbours were always changing. In Pwll, the next-door neighbour has a permanent key. He is a builder always doing work for them. The builder also speaks of the time he himself spent near London working in the building trade, finding it difficult to come to terms with the on-site racism he encountered. He can't understand how Tony and Catriona can live in such an environment.

Catriona also loves it all. She has spent her own life being here, there and everywhere, and really appreciates now being part of a more close-knit community.

Her father was born in Yorkshire of Scottish descent, her mother was Dutch. Her father spent the war as an engineer based in India, her mother working for the Red Cross in Canada. Her father also obtained an economics degree from Harvard, and met Catriona's mother in Washington DC where he had moved to work.

Both Catriona and her sister were born in Washington, before moving to the UK when Catriona was six, Catriona going to primary school in Watford. Her father then joined Glaxo and was posted to Bombay. Catriona's secondary education involved both a European school in Bombay and a boarding school in Switzerland.

She then trained to become a primary school teacher in Roehampton, and spent the last twelve years of her working life running a special-needs unit for Hounslow local authority.

Leading such a diverse life all over the globe, Catriona was initially quite taken aback by the friendliness and warmth of her Llanelli welcome. A welcome also incidentally given to a Polish friend who accompanied Catriona and Tony to Wales for the previously-mentioned family christening.

Tony's working career in the civil service also initially took him in rapid succession to Anglesey, then Swansea, before London. His last eleven years were spent as a conciliation officer for ACAS.

And as both Tony's and Catriona's early lives had been so hectic, neither had in fact found the time to learn to drive. And in any case, in London a car can be as much a hindrance as a benefit.

In Llanelli, however, there is always a friend on hand to provide transport, a facility unlikely to be available to them if they had moved to France. And Llanelli is also far more generally accessible from London. And this is important given they have got into the habit of visiting West Wales every two or three weeks, mainly it should be said to watch the Scarlets' home games. Tony is a season ticket holder of both London Welsh and Scarlets. So the last remaining factor in their preference for Pwll over Provence is a love of rugby and the Scarlets. Although I wonder whether they would not have found an equally-suitable retreat near Toulon!

The attraction of Llanelli is social rather than connected to nationalism or culture. He enjoys meeting old friends from his schooldays. Neighbours are always ringing up or popping in.

Many of his friends have never left Llanelli, and they have probably lived in the same houses all their married lives. They are fervently nationalistic, clearly demonstrated in their support for Wales in rugby. For Tony, however, being Welsh is not crucial. Forty-one years in the civil service has made him somewhat apolitical.

But he wouldn't want not to be Welsh. He reads the *Western Mail*, and listens to Welsh choirs both on S4C and frequently at Llanelli's new Theatr Ffwrnes. And he and Catriona spent the whole week at the National Eistedddfod when it was last held in Llanelli in 2014. In readiness for the 2015 Rugby World Cup, Catriona even learned the words of the Welsh national anthem, a task she didn't actually find too demanding given her knowledge of languages acquired residing in every corner of the globe.

According to Tony's census form he is Welsh, and he claims he would have voted Yes in 1999. He approves of bilingual signposts and leaflets, and of Welsh-language education. He believes in the Assembly, although feels it needs more funding, and thinks that Wales would struggle if completely independent.

But his heart belongs to the local community. Irrespective of town-planning failures, problems with drugs, and the need to assimilate large scale immigration, he loves the banter, the networking and the reminiscences of sport and schooldays. 'Once a Llanelli boy, always a Llanelli boy.'

Roger Banner

Roger Banner was a contemporary of mine in what used to be the University College of Wales, Aberystwyth, during the early 1960s. We weren't close friends in college, but our paths crossed again during the 1980s as keen supporters of the London Welsh RFC at Old Deer Park in Richmond.

Roger was born in Caerleon and grew up in Newport in what was then called Wales and Monmouthshire. His father was a road design engineer. He attended Newport High School, and read geography and geology at Aberystwyth. To quote Roger himself, after three years as a student, 'he was both relieved and grateful to have been awarded a degree.'

government a newspaper or TV article is discussing. And as there is more than likely to be an English focus, the Welsh population can quite easily draw wrong conclusions about what government actions apply to Wales, or what policies the Welsh Assembly are adopting.

But at least in Llantwit one is definitely in Wales. You have only to watch a rugby match in the rugby club bar to be aware of this. I claim that I only moved to Wales to get away from the hype surrounding the 2015 Rugby World Cup in England. Given the early English demise I almost wish I'd stayed for the fun.

In London pubs I always felt I was viewed as different by fellow drinkers, most of whom had never been to Wales, or even knew of its precise location or extent.

But with the cultural and economic dominance of our neighbours, in Wales itself one is also made to feel part of a much larger British whole. We have English neighbours. Many Welsh families have relations living in England. Local businessmen frequently travel into England on business. And holidaymakers fly, not only from Cardiff, but from Bristol, Heathrow and even Gatwick.

All this leads to less sense of division, but doesn't do much for either the Welsh economy or the cause of Welsh nationalism.

And the Welsh, as ever, are fairly apathetic about politics. I have constantly griped about not being able, in England, to vote on matters affecting Wales. Now that I live here, arriving in time to vote in the 2016 Welsh Assembly elections, I was slightly ambivalent about what to do with my vote.

Voting at local level is not a problem, with the town council dominated by an affiliation of independent candidates operating under the title of 'Llantwit First Independents' with the slogan 'Putting People Before Politics'. Brilliant. Although it remains to be seen whether the party can also influence the more important Vale of Glamorgan Borough Council.

As far as Assembly politics are concerned, I feel the Labour

Government seem to have made some progress of late, but the consensus amongst my sample of returning exiles is that, over the long term, Labour have been close to a disaster, and to some extent have only themselves to blame for initially creating an Assembly with such limited powers. Blair never wanted it to succeed. The Tories, as the party in power in Westminster, then recently produced a Wales Bill which failed to increase these powers, and in a style typical of both Cameron's and Theresa May's governments, were forced to reconsider their recommendations. The Lib Dems are unfortunately non-existent, and Plaid Cymru suddenly turned childish, voting against an e-cigarette bill merely because a Labour politician was rude to them in the Assembly.

Finally there is UKIP. Apart from the fact that Wales needed every grant it could get out of Europe, I find the whole concept of a party which attempts to perpetuate an English way of life a total irrelevance. The perpetuation of a British way of life seems more relevant than clinging on to a sense of Welshness.

So in true Welsh style I am in danger of becoming apathetic about politics. Just living life the Welsh way seems in itself much more relevant and important.

And every morning we stand in the kitchen looking out at our lovely backdrop of fields and horses, with my wife Gill exclaiming how much she continues to love the house, the people and the area.

And family and friends are forever being invited down to visit us.

So there you are then. Wales *is* a paradise on Earth.

Postscript

THE FRENCH PHILOSOPHER René Descartes once pronounced that 'I think, therefore I am'.

This profound observation equates to my feeling of Welshness. I feel Welsh, I have a sense of Welshness, of being different. Therefore such a thing as a Welsh identity must exist.

Critics might argue that Welshness means different things to different people; different to a North Walian than to a South Walian, different in rural compared to urban areas, different for an exile compared to a resident. But there are many constant characteristics which I and many of my countrymen claim to recognise and to which we aspire.

The Welshman's self-image encompasses elements of passion, friendliness, humour, music, rugby, classlessness and radicalism.

Perhaps the sense of greater friendliness is a rural-versus-urban phenomenon. On holiday recently in England's Peak District, on the cusp between Staffordshire and Derbyshire, I was also struck by the friendliness of the 'natives'. Fellow golfers readily passed the time of day, bestowing me with such titles as 'squire' and 'you beaut'!

Or in Britain is it more specifically a function of living anywhere but London?

In Wales at least, community friendliness also extends out of rural environments into the urban and post-industrial South Wales Valleys.

And even Dan Boucher, ex-Conservative candidate for the National Assembly, argues in his book *The Big Society in a Small Country: Wales, Social Capital, Mutualism and Self-Help* that 'not only is the Big Society relevant to Wales in the sense of providing much needed practical policy solutions to pressing problems, it actually has the potential to achieve a far better fit with Welsh than English culture.

'When considered in the context of the broad sweep of history, Wales is often characterised as a "community of communities", a nation and culture best understood from the bottom up than from the top down. The cultural roots for this go way back, finding expression in the fact that, although Wales enjoyed a nationwide law from the eighth century, it actually struggled with the idea of a common executive and was for the most part ruled by a series of different princes covering their own patches of Wales. When Wales was then annexed to England and there was no "Welsh" government as such and the Welsh language was banned in all contexts apart from church and chapel, there was a real sense in which Wales withdrew into a church and chapel which came to be dominated by non-conformity, which was again characterised by a profound decentralisation.'

Dan Boucher tempers this philosophy by also arguing that such a Big Society has, in the twentieth century, become overshadowed by Labour's Big State, with a public sector that still today represents what he sees as a frightening 70% of the economy.

Be that as it may, the Big Society has, in many districts of England, given licence to local businesses, especially developers and estate agents, to ride roughshod over planning regulations, and go in search of profit whatever the consequences to the local environment, all in the name of 'the man in the street'. In my previous local Hertfordshire vicinity, they are building not starter homes but more and more mansions for the super rich, usually in the back gardens of existing homes. The Big Society has become a licence to flout community rules rather than help it meet its needs.

Observers claim that Wales has far less class division. If snobbishness exists it is to be found amongst those set on becoming more anglicised. Hence our love of deflating pomposity, our dislike of the *crach* or *crachach*, the so-called upper class. The downside of this tendency is that we almost discourage personal as opposed to intellectual or creative ambition, and are innately suspicious of anyone with wealth or power, especially our own Welsh politicians.

And whilst the Welsh have strong liberal and radical tendencies, a belief in equal opportunity for everyone, this has seldom translated itself into a drive for their own independence. To refer again to the view expressed by travel writer Jan Morris, 'the Welsh have seldom suffered from national ambition, only national grievance'.

This has partly been engendered by the society in which we have lived, a society dominated by the English, who over the centuries have encouraged the dismissal of all things passing as Welsh.

The Laws of Union in the sixteenth century ostensibly gave Welshmen the same rights as Englishmen, but these were only of benefit if you spoke English and moved closer to London.

From the mid-nineteenth century, English became the language of the classroom, resulting in only 20% of today's population speaking Welsh, the same percentage that had spoken English in 1850. And the British government can't even now be bothered to monitor how many in England also speak Welsh.

All road and rail links were focussed on getting to England, with almost non-existent links between North and South Wales, and the new twentieth-century media of radio and television initially, in both content and regional structure, gave zero recognition to the existence of Wales.

The people of Wales came too easily to accept this scenario. American author Noah Hawley, in his novel *The Good Father*, writes about moving his family to California to be able to visit his son sentenced to death for assassinating the US President elect. Weekdays were spent in ordinary family life, every weekend was taken up by prison visits. He reflects: 'I was amazed that the human animal could, over time, come to define any situation, no matter how unnatural, as normal.'

So it was in Wales from 1850 for 100 years.

But Wales has finally responded.

Ironically Descartes's 'I think therefore I am' takes on an even greater appropriateness and significance in our understanding of my sense of Welshness. Descartes's awareness of the existence of self stems originally from questioning his own existence. Doubting one's existence, in and of itself, proves that an 'I' exists to do the thinking. While other knowledge could be a figment of imagination, deception or mistake, the very act of doubting one's own existence arguably serves as proof of one's own existence, or at least of one's thought. So it is with Wales.

With no hold on government or economy, a sense of Welshness has been preserved via the more ephemeral values of language, voice, a sense of humanity, and even support for the Welsh rugby team.

In all matters there has always been a tinge of self-doubt, felt most acutely in matters of language. The non-Welsh speaking majority have often questioned the rights of the *Cymry Cymraeg*, but well-known writers and broadcasters Ned Thomas and Trevor Fishlock argue succinctly that there is no credence whatsoever to the argument that the efforts to promote the Welsh language are misplaced because they work on behalf of a mere 20% minority. Such promotion is totally acceptable purely as a matter of democracy. Every minority have an unquestioned right to preserve their language and culture.

And it is this minority of Welsh speakers who have been most proactive in resurrecting our Welsh identity over the last sixty or so years, from Tryweryn, via bilingual road signs to S4C and a Welsh Assembly in Cardiff Bay. And they have carried much of the remaining population along with them. In 1962 in Aberystwyth University, I dismissed the road block on Pont Trefechan by *Cymdeithas yr Iaith Gymraeg* (the Welsh Language Society) as the work of extremists. I now feel an amazing sense of pride and identity when the first sight of a bilingual road sign tells me that I have entered Wales, and in politics I am very much a federalist.

But Welshness is not dependent on being able to speak Welsh, nor even on living in Wales. Welsh exiles in fact seem to feel the pull of Welshness more than the indigenous population, and have been responsible for much of the drive towards a greater sense of identity. Lloyd George and R S Thomas, for example, were both of Welsh parents, but born in England.

Yet American Pamela Petro, who studied Welsh in Lampeter, claims that 'the desire to learn Welsh is all about place. I can't imagine wanting to learn Welsh without knowing Wales.'

Many of us feel this need to experience Wales itself again. But as this book has illustrated, much has changed over the last half a century.

We have much more of a sense of identity, with a National Assembly and a language that is far more alive. We also possess an economy that is struggling, and a social environment which, whilst far more progressive and lively, is in danger of becoming anonymous with the globalisation and increasing mobility of the modern world.

We can but hope that we are not so apathetic as to passively accept the limited powers so far given to the National Assembly, and that the politicians in Cardiff Bay give us a body of which we can be proud and which is equipped to turn around the fortunes of our post-industrial economy.

Even if we fail, we must still take responsibility for our own welfare to ensure that the needs of Wales are given conscious consideration in the UK political and economic process.

And in this world of increasing globalisation, we must preserve traditional Welsh values and culture. The UK may be a civilised country with a lively media and entertainment scene, but there is still room for things Welsh, particularly with regard to human values.

The existence of different individual cultures provides variety and humanity, a counter-culture, in the face of the 'crushing uniformity' of current life. We must squash the belief that preserving an ancient heritage is necessarily backward- rather than forward-looking.

And Trevor Fishlock adds: 'The modern emphasis is on economic growth, centralisation, large corporations and bureaucracies, and the inclination to examine human endeavour in terms of profit and usefulness, which tends to push individual and community needs and feelings into the background. Respect for people and their dignity has been lessened.' Such respect must be preserved.

Our returning exiles must play their part, however small. They must give something back.

They are not all so inclined. Most are in the latter stages of life. They may be after an easy life. They sit in the Welsh equivalent of the Thames Valley outside of the disintegrating urban scene. But they mostly feel Welsh and not English. They are Welsh first, British second. And they would want the clan to survive, whatever its form.

I will leave the last words to another foreigner. Imogen Rhia Herrad was born and grew up in Germany, and apparently like many of her compatriots had a fascination for all things Celtic. As I mentioned much earlier in the book, she spent a year in Britain as a foreign language assistant, choosing rural Wales as a location, and in the space of a week, had 'fallen utterly in love with the place'. She enrolled on a two-month intensive Welsh summer course, and then spent a year teaching German in the schools of Aberystwyth, with the Welsh language coming in handy to gain the respect of the children in the classroom.

This was when she heard about the Welsh in Patagonia, and began to dream of going there just to see what it was like. She has subsequently visited there on countless occasions, and become fascinated not only by the story of the Welsh settlers, but in the forbidding landscape and by the history and fate of the South American native peoples who originally inhabited these lands. She has written about her many visits in her book *Beyond the Pampas: In Search of Patagonia*, recalling how, when first meeting with Argentinian ancestors of the first Welsh settlers, the only option was to converse through the

descendents?

medium of Welsh, as she couldn't speak Spanish, and they had no command of English or German.

On 28 May 1865 the *Mimosa*, with 153 Welsh men, women and children on board, set sail for Patagonia, to start a new life away from the hegemony of the English Government which they felt was threatening their language, their religion and the very fabric of their identity.

Today there are estimated to be 50,000 of Welsh descent in the three main settlements in *Y Wladfa* (The Colony), although only about 10% are Welsh speakers. The Welsh settlers in fact experienced similar difficulties in dealing with the Argentinian government to those they had had with Westminster, and have had to fight hard to ensure Welsh is taught in schools and spoken in the chapels.

Since 1965 and the celebration of the centenary of the first voyage, Wales itself has shown more interest in preserving the Welshness of the colony, and the speaking of Welsh has become more of a desirable commodity there with the growing Welsh tourist trade.

But the treatment of the Welsh settlers by the Argentinian government diminishes to nothing in comparison to the manner in which the same government decimated the lives of the various indigenous native tribes.

Whilst these indigenous tribes suffered far more than the Welsh, one can draw a parallel, in that they, like the Welsh, are now attempting to preserve their identity through culture and language. And the joy that Imogen expresses on witnessing this resurgence is encouragement and even proof that it may all be worth the effort.

'It's an unfamiliar vision of the world to me. I'm the product of an individualistic society. I come from an abusive family. I have no family now, there are no ancestors that I care about.

'But now, for the first time, I see that the enmeshedness of a clan need not be suffocating, entrapping, hampering. It can be empowering. It can give one's struggles meaning.'

By the same author: